# MISFITS AND MARBLE FAUNS

MERCER
UNIVERSITY PRESS

*Endowed by*
TOM WATSON BROWN
*and*
THE WATSON-BROWN FOUNDATION, INC.

# MISFITS AND MARBLE FAUNS

## RELIGION AND ROMANCE IN HAWTHORNE AND O'CONNOR

Wendy Piper

MERCER UNIVERSITY PRESS

MACON, GEORGIA

MUP/H816

© 2011 Mercer University Press
1400 Coleman Avenue
Macon, Georgia 31207
All rights reserved

First Edition

Books published by Mercer University Press are printed on acid-free paper that
meets the requirements of American National Standard for Information
Sciences—Permanence of Paper for Printed Library Materials.

Mercer University Press is a member of Green Press Initiative
(greenpressinitiative.org), a nonprofit organization working to help publishers
and printers increase their use of recycled paper and decrease their use of fiber
derived from endangered forests. This book is printed on recycled paper.
ISBN      978-0-88146-217-3
Cataloging-in-Publication Data is available from the Library of Congress


Library of Congress Cataloging-in-Publication Data
Piper, Wendy, 1960- Misfits and marble fauns : religion and romance in
Hawthorne and O'Connor / Wendy Piper. -- 1st ed.
p. cm.
Includes bibliographical references and index.
ISBN 978-0-88146-217-3 (hardcover : alk. paper)
1. Hawthorne, Nathaniel, 1804-1864--Criticism and interpretation.
2. Hawthorne, Nathaniel, 1804-1864--Religion. 3. O'Connor, Flannery--
Criticism and interpretation. 4. O'Connor, Flannery--Religion. 5. Religion in
literature. 6. Love stories, American--History and criticism. I. Title.
PS1892.R4P56 2011
813'.3--dc22
                                                      2011002081

*To Julie*

*and*

*to Howard*

*Friend and Mentor*

# CONTENTS

# PREFACE

Some years ago, when I began graduate school, I was given an assignment for a course in Literary Criticism. The assignment asked that I research an author who was both "a poet and critic," "poet" being understood broadly in Aristotelian terms as a "maker" of poetry or fiction. As I worked to narrow my focus, my instructor helped me by asking whose fiction I enjoyed. Given my interest in short fiction, as well as in philosophy and religion, I answered that I had always enjoyed the short stories of Flannery O'Connor. He responded by going to his bookcase and handing me a copy of *The Habit of Being*. This introduction to O'Connor's fiction and prose began an enthusiasm for the mind and work of an author that is still going strong some twenty-odd years later. As the years passed and I read and taught more of the works of Hawthorne, I noticed the strong affinity between them in terms of vision and material that O'Connor so frequently remarks on. I noticed, as well, the pleasure that my students took in reading such tales of Hawthorne as "My Kinsman, Major Molineau" and "Young Goodman Brown," when paired with O'Connor's "The Artificial Nigger" and "Good Country People." The development of such traditional themes associated with American romance as alienation and redemption, freedom and self-renewal, were particularly interesting when considered within O'Connor's twentieth-century cultural context.

I was also attracted to O'Connor's Catholicism, both as it informed her work and as it gave meaning and purpose to her life. I read and reread *The Habit of Being*, laughing out loud as I sat alone in the college cafeteria at her wicked sense of humor. As others have remarked, and O'Connor herself has pointed out, her strong faith gave her the ability to look at the most serious situations, both personal and beyond, with self-deprecating humor and wry wit. More and more, however, as I pored through the letters and essays, I was intrigued by her insistence that her stories stand alone, and that the moral vision supplied by her Catholic belief be conveyed solely through the integrity of her art itself. Aided by my teacher, Howard Pearce, a literary critic well versed in trends in twentieth-century philosophy, I began to notice similarities between O'Connor's sacramental sense—her insistence on the concrete—and the claims of such philosophers as Edmund Husserl, Martin Heidegger, and Hans-Georg Gadamer. Their work in phenomenology and hermeneutics argued that knowledge is to be gained through sensory experience, through our return to phenomena, or to things themselves. This insistence on experience rather than abstraction sought to reconcile the age-old rift between subject and object; truth was to be found—not in the ideal or in the actual—but in the reconciliation of the two, or in experience. Here, I believed, was a fresh lens through which to view O'Connor's critique of the destructive dualism of modernity that existed outside of religious and theological approaches to her fiction. Against the claims of modern subjectivism, philosophical hermeneutics offered an aesthetic that would assert the integrity of art itself and the truth claims of aesthetic experience. It would therefore offer a new understanding of the ethical interest that lay behind O'Connor's own sacramental vision.

All of this led me back to Hawthorne. It is his formulation of the romance that O'Connor calls upon in her articulation of the grotesque. As he asserts the "truth of the human heart"[1] as being the subject of his fiction, Hawthorne declares the domain of the romance to be a "neutral territory"[2] that frees his fiction from the claims to objectivity of literary realism, and as it blends inner and

---

[1] Nathaniel Hawthorne, preface to *The House of the Seven Gables,* in vol 2, *The Centenary Edition of the Works of Nathaniel Hawthorne* (Columbus: Ohio State University Press, 1965) vii.

[2] ———, "The Custom House," in *The Scarlet Letter* in vol. 1, *The Centenary Edition of the Works of Nathaniel Hawthorne* (Columbus: Ohio State University Press, 1962) 36.

outer reality, the romance form closes the gap between subject and object upon which modern scientific objectivity is based. The central experience of each of these writers, then, is that of mystery. In a similar way, Gadamer's assertion of the dialogic nature of understanding, as well as his notion of the philosophical nature of art, call into question the sovereignty of modern scientific rationalism. Like Hawthorne and O'Connor, Gadamer demonstrates that aesthetic experience results in the recognition of the fundamental finitude of human being and knowing.

For each of these writers, the humility of genuine self-knowledge is asserted against the prevailing subjectivism of modernity. My hope in bringing the insights of philosophical hermeneutics to bear on the work of these writers of American romance is to celebrate their artistic vision and the moral dimension that underlies it.

# Acknowledgments

I am grateful to many people for helping me bring this project to completion. I wish first to thank Tom Cormen, Professor of Computer Science and former Director of the Institute for Writing and Rhetoric at Dartmouth College, for his generous support throughout this process. My friend and colleague Michael Chaney of the English Department at Dartmouth has provided me with encouragement and practical advice along the way. He has helped me remember the importance of clarity and concision in my prose. I wish to thank Bill Sessions for his friendship and encouragement, and for his comments on early portions of my manuscript—our ongoing conversations are a delight to me. I want to thank Ralph Wood for his friendship as well; in a variety of milieus, he has challenged my thinking and reading of O'Connor in ways that have helped me to become a more thorough and demanding critic. I'm grateful to my students who have enjoyed reading Hawthorne and O'Connor with me. I appreciate the energy and insight they've brought to our conversations. Finally, and most of all, I owe my deepest gratitude to Howard D. Pearce. He fostered me as a graduate student, challenged my thinking, and led me to new levels of scholarship. Howard left us a few years ago, and I have missed him dearly during the final phases of this project. Though I would have benefited immeasurably from conversations with him, his spirit fills the pages of this book.

# ABBREVIATIONS

*CW*  Flannery O'Connor. *Collected Works of Flannery O'Connor*. Edited by Sally Fitzgerald. New York: Library of America, 1988.

*HB*  Flannery O'Connor. *The Habit of Being: Letters of Flannery O'Connor*. Edited by Sally Fitzgerald. New York: Farrar, Straus and Giroux, 1979.

*MM*  Flannery O'Connor. *Mystery and Manners: Occasional Prose*. Edited by Sally and Robert Fitzgerald. New York: Farrar, Straus and Giroux, 1969.

# INTRODUCTION

Throughout her letters and critical essays, Flannery O'Connor cites Hawthorne as both a kindred spirit and an influence on her work. In a letter to William Sessions, dated 13 September 1960, she states unequivocally that, as a writer of "romances," she is one of Hawthorne's "descendants"; likewise, she writes later to John Hawkes that she feels "more of a kinship with [Hawthorne] than with any other American ..." (*HB* 407, 457). From what we can glean from the letters—one to a friend and college professor, the other to a contemporary fiction writer—O'Connor seemed anxious to clear up possible misunderstandings of her work and purpose. According to the letters, William Sessions tended toward a psychoanalytical reading of O'Connor's fiction—he is notoriously rebuked by her in an earlier letter for seeing Freudian symbols where she claims none were intended (*CW* 1130–31). John Hawkes, whose own command of the grotesque O'Connor greatly admired, at least once in the letters cast her as a Romantic, and, like Sessions, seemed predisposed toward the secular and the rational in his interpretations of her characters. By calling upon her affinity with Hawthorne, then, O'Connor seemed determined to place herself within the American romance tradition, as Hawthorne distinguishes it from that of the novel, and as it rests on fundamental assumptions that neither he nor O'Connor would identify as Romantic.

As Hawthorne defines the romance form for American fiction, he frees it from the novelistic criterion of social verisimilitude demanded by literary realism and naturalism. Within the context of the American literary tradition, he grants the writer of fiction the freedom to explore the range of the possible, not the probable, and to investigate the subject of human nature, to explore the domain of a mysterious moral inner realm. The writer of romance thus tends away from the narrow realm of the actual demanded by realism in order to represent the universal "truth of the human heart."

Hawthorne's interest in moral nature, in conflict and contradiction, is in sharp contrast to the liberal spirit of the Romantic era and of the scientific and expansionist vision of the nineteenth century in general. Indeed, his difference from his contemporaries is evident in his critique of the progressive sensibility of the Transcendentalists. Their Romantic faith in the forward march of humanity, underscored by Emerson's conviction, set forth in "Nature," of the ultimate transparency of nature, suggested to Hawthorne an idealism that was both naïve and dangerous. As this idealism dismissed the reality of evil and suffering from human experience—as such sketches as "Earth's Holocaust" and "The Celestial Rail-road" make clear—it diminished the integrity or the reality of the world outside the self. The material world is thus subjectified; it becomes inconsequential, expendable—or at least amenable to mind—in the name of reform and progress.

The same subjectivism that issues from the imbalance of head and heart distinguishes, for Hawthorne, modern scientific or dichotomous thinking, generally. It, therefore, characterizes not only his parodies of idealist philosophers of the nineteenth century, but also his representations of scientists and other like-minded theoreticians. Thus, while characters such as Aylmer and Rappaccini submit the delicate material world—the fleshly existence of their wives and daughters—to the investigatory and objectifying gaze of their science, the Puritans attempt to mold the material world in order to achieve their earthly utopia. The Puritans' progressive scheme of the seventeenth century is thus shown to be as scientistic as that of Hawthorne's nineteenth-century professional scientists and social engineers, based, as it is, in the ultimate knowability of, and hence control over, nature and human nature that reason affords. As a result, Hawthorne shows such idealism, whether scientific or religious (and Hawthorne's portrayal of the religious enthusiasm of his nineteenth-century scientists would suggest that it is both), results in a subjectivism that, as it privileges the knowing mind over matter, objectifies the world outside the self. The scientifically minded theoretician—a Chillingworth or Ethan Brand—holds himself aloof from human relations, assumes a "self-relying intelligence," and from this standpoint outside of history, comes to know, and ultimately to control, material being. Such an act of abstraction, characteristic of the artist figure, the scientist, and also of the liberal reformer as social scientist, diminishes the worth of the world and of human community as well, as it seeks to transcend the limitations of the material world and history.

Against this presumption of the modern scientific sensibility, Hawthorne asserts the complex "truth of the human heart" as both the reality of human nature and as the subject of his fiction. "Boundless" and divided, as he describes it—the "mesh of good and evil"[1] that characterizes Hester Prynne—it calls for a mode of representation that suggests its unknowability. Hawthorne's conception of romance, therefore, suggests a "neutral territory," a twilight region between the ideal and the actual, that blurs the distinction between inner and outer reality and collapses the dichotomy between subject and object upon which modern scientific objectivity is founded. Hawthorne's representative characters, then, his young and naïve Puritans, aspiring artists, and scientifically minded theoreticians, are often recalled, through a process of discovery characteristic of the romance as genre, to an apprehension of the mystery at the heart of existence, and thus to an awareness of the limitations of their human nature. At the least, they witness the failure of their idealistic projects of reform; at best, they are restored to a sense of humanity and place within human community.

---

[1] Hawthorne, *The Scarlet Letter*, 64.

It is this "truth of the human heart," the reality of our divided or "fallen" state in Christian terms, that O'Connor refers to when she cites the material of the "dark and divisive" American romance tradition as the subject of her own fiction (*MM* 46). Sharing an interest with Hawthorne in the "old Adam,"[2] O'Connor describes the topic of good fiction as human nature, and within her Catholic Christian context, the mystery implicit in the "truth of the human heart" becomes the mystery surrounding human nature and existence, generally. She thus defines the central conflict of her own romance-novels as the assertion of "free will," or the struggle of conflicting wills within the free individual, and she explains that the representation of such a conflict exceeds the bounds of modern rationalistic thinking and thus of literary realism and naturalism. As O'Connor's fiction defies the expectations of modern rationalism, Hawthorne's genre of romance becomes O'Connor's grotesque, and her characterizations of maimed individuals suggest, from a Christian perspective, the mystery or incompleteness inherent in human life.

Following Hawthorne, then, O'Connor's fiction evokes not only the mystery of human existence, but also the finitude of human being and knowing that this mystery implies. She asserts the reality of this mystery—dramatized not only by her grotesque characters, but also by the violent intrusions of grace into their lives—against what she similarly perceives to be the rationalism and dualism inherent in the modern sensibility. Writing from within a Christian context, however, O'Connor identifies and dramatizes the root of this dualism as well as its consequences. She characterizes modernity, since the Enlightenment, in terms of its decreasing dependence upon God and an increasing faith in humanistic endeavor, enabled by our confidence in reason. Such Enlightenment rationalism, as it has banished God from the world,

---

[2] Rosemary M. Magee, ed., *Conversations with Flannery O'Connor*, Literary Conversations Series (Jackson: University Press of Mississippi, 1987) 99.

has desacralized creation, and reason has thus become deracinated, or cut loose from being itself. Lacking this recognition of a common divine source, the secular deracinated intellect identifies thought with all of creation, and reduces material being to an abstraction that is manipulable by mind. Hawthorne's scientific sensibility thus becomes, for O'Connor, the secular, autonomous intellect that, having banished grace from nature, assumes unmitigated power over creation and is therefore characterized by its will-to-power. Its secularity, in the mid-twentieth century, has, further, assumed the shape of nihilism. Therefore, just as O'Connor's rationalists assume a theoretical mindset, attempting to reform the world by means of the ability granted them by reason, her intelligent nihilists seek to bend the worthless world to fit their own schemes of meaning.

The rationalism and dualism of Enlightenment modernity, then, has as dire consequences for O'Connor as it does for Hawthorne. Consequently, as a writer who wrote much about the nature of fiction, O'Connor explains the influence that her sacramental vision has on her art. Drawing from Hawthorne's formulation of a "neutral territory," she explains that the artist distorts the real, or the natural, in order to convey her vision. The work of art is thus understood to be independent of external reality; because it combines both the inner and outer worlds, it becomes an autonomous whole, and our experience of it is one of an encounter that yields a sense of mystery. Similarly, O'Connor explains that her narrative technique is intended to undermine our modern rationalism. As the sacraments of her theology point to the mystery that surrounds existence, and as the Catholic Eucharist reveals the grace that inheres in matter, her sacramental sense determines what she calls an "incarnational," or dramatic, theory of fiction. Her intention to dramatize the mystery inherent in our existence thus likens her form and vision to that of tragic drama. It suggests that as a writer of romance, she shares with her American forbear a tragic vision that she embodies in form. She wishes to

5

convey the fundamental finitude of our existence and hence to offer a critique of our aims toward rational self-sufficiency.

The fiction of Hawthorne and O'Connor can best be understood and enhanced through an understanding of Gadamer's hermeneutics. His work in interpretation theory revises traditional thinking about the hermeneutical process of understanding and interpretation in such a way as to move beyond the subject/object dichotomy of modern methodological thought. Against the scientific model of understanding that removes the knowing subject from history in order to obtain the ideal of objective knowledge—and in doing so, reduces "the world to an object of investigation and control"—Gadamer argues that the achievement of understanding occurs in a fusion of perspectives or horizons.[3] His revision of traditional hermeneutical thinking undermines the subjectivism of modern method, and, as it reveals the conversational, and hence temporal, nature of our understanding, it points to the fundamental finitude of human knowing and being. The aim of Gadamer's hermeneutics, then, while it speaks specifically to theories of interpretation within the human sciences, is to critique and ultimately to undermine the will-to-power over creation that he argues is inherent in modern scientistic thinking.

Drawing from a contemporary philosophical framework, this study traces key concepts in the American romance tradition that are increasingly relevant today. In the light of global terror, the romance genre asserts the dark and complicated truth of the human heart against the certainties that underlie the rationalism of modern liberalism as well as the nihilism represented in O'Connor's fiction. The first few chapters of the book thereby undertake to define the conflict between head and heart of Hawthorne's romance that he asserts against the prevailing optimism of such

---

[3] David E. Linge, introduction to *Philosophical Hermeneutics,* by Hans-Georg Gadamer, trans. David E. Linge (Berkeley: University of California Press, 1977) xli.

contemporaries as Emerson and extends the analysis of Hawthorne's "neutral territory" to include Gadamer's critique of the subjectivism that underlies modernity. Hawthorne's dramatization of the damage inflicted upon their victims by such detached scientist and artist figures as Chillingworth, Aylmer, and Ethan Brand suggests Gadamer's contemporary critique of the objectifying methodology of modern science.

In chapter one, I investigate the historical and cultural context of Hawthorne's mid-nineteenth-century formulation of the romance and demonstrate the affinity between Hawthorne's generic definition of the romance as co-implication of subject and object and Gadamer's critique of modern method in *The Blithedale Romance, The House of the Seven Gables,* and several short stories. The imbalance of head and heart characteristic of Hawthorne's artist/idealists and scientists is shown to prefigure Gadamer's critique of the aesthetic consciousness. Chapter two develops this equation between the isolated intellect and Gadamer's description of the modern dichotomous mindset as it occurs in Hawthorne's characterization of the Puritans in *The Scarlet Letter.* In their confidence that they can ascertain the truth of Hester Prynne's heart, I argue that the Puritan magistrates exhibit the objectifying methodology of modern science that defines progress as knowledge of nature for the purpose of control. Similarly, in her attempt to evade the law, Hester herself privileges mind over matter and denies the reality of the historical world. I, therefore, treat the traditional dichotomies in the novel as instances of the modern subjective sensibility. Chapter three argues that as *The Marble Faun,* Hawthorne's last romance, follows the process of self-discovery characteristic of the genre in the development of the characters of Hilda and Donatello, it dramatizes the hermeneutical concept of "Bildung," in which self-discovery is shown to be a historical, dialogic process. I demonstrate that as Hilda grows in self-awareness, she moves from a Platonic insistence on the work of art as merely copy, to an Aristotelian understanding of the truth claim of aesthetic experience. Such an understanding posits tragedy and human limit rather than idealism as central to the human experience.

In chapter four, I continue the critique of the scientific rationalism of modern culture offered by Hawthorne and Gadamer from the standpoint of O'Connor's religious and artistic vision and practice. I draw from O'Connor's letters and essays as well as her fiction to demonstrate her transformation of Hawthorne's formulation of the romance in her use of the grotesque and argue that her own sacramental aesthetics evoke Gadamer's assertion of the historicality of human being and knowing. I offer a reading of *The Violent Bear It Away* as a romance in which the hero Tarwater must choose between the life of reason or imagination. Following insights of Gadamer, I argue that his ultimate choice determines a sacramental over a scientistic relationship to the world. In chapter five, I investigate the evolution of Hawthorne's idealists to O'Connor's rationalist/nihilist of the mid-twentieth century. I examine the journey of the young nihilist Hazel Motes in *Wise Blood* and explore the social and metaphysical consequences of the deracinated intellect in "Good Country People," "The Displaced Person," and "Revelation." Against the subjectivism of modernity, the characters in each of these stories come to recognize that an experience of finitude is the required ground for self-knowledge. Following O'Connor's reflections on the nature of fiction and art as well as those of Gadamer, I argue that the reader undergoes a similar experience. Through an encounter with the work of art, the domain of reason is surpassed in an experience of mystery. In the final chapter, I argue that the essential mystery that both Hawthorne and O'Connor claim to be at the heart of the romance as genre is shared by the form and vision of tragedy. Following insights of the twentieth-century phenomenological movement in philosophy, I demonstrate the affinity between the romance tradition and O'Connor's sacramental aesthetics that will lead to a return to the world of sensory experience and to a dramatic theory of fiction. I offer a reading of O'Connor's fiction and criticism in terms of these dramatic, and ultimately tragic, elements inherent in her narrative technique. The chapter concludes with a discussion of Martha Nussbaum's analysis of the ethics of tragic recognition, which, as demonstrated by O'Connor's use of violence, rests on a passional versus rational response to the drama. The truth claim of art explored in chapters three and five is thus concluded in this final chapter as I argue that characters and reader are shown a universal dimension of human experience that is not available through the method of modern science.

While some studies have been done of the critical and artistic lineage of Hawthorne and O'Connor, I believe that this interdisciplinary grouping renders new insight into the significance of their generic and thematic similarities as they are conceived in the context of developments in contemporary philosophical hermeneutics.[4] In bringing both Hawthorne and

---

[4] The artistic kinship between Hawthorne and O'Connor is widely acknowledged, though it has not been studied in depth. Virginia Wray argues for the inclusion of O'Connor within the "dark tradition" of American romance on the basis of her skepticism regarding American liberal values ("Flannery O'Connor in the American Romance Tradition," 84). Similarly, Emily Budick argues, perhaps against the grain of some feminist criticism, that O'Connor's fictional intent aligns her with the male-dominated romance tradition that she characterizes as "fundamentally skepticist" (*Engendering Romance: Women Writers and the Hawthorne Tradition 1850–1990*, 4). Mary Gordon has recently noted that the anti-bourgeois aspect of O'Connor's fiction aligns her with romance rather than with prose fiction, which is bourgeois in its origins ("Is Flannery O'Connor a Catholic?" 1). Frederick Asals notes ties between O'Connor and both Poe and Hawthorne and remarks a strong similarity between *The Violent Bear It Away* and *The Scarlet Letter* (*Flannery O'Connor: The Imagination of Extremity*), as do Leon Driskell and Joan Brittain in *The Eternal Crossroads*. Samuel Coale argues that while both Hawthorne and O'Connor portray dark Manichean worlds devoid of grace, O'Connor's Catholic vision offers redemption, whereas Hawthorne's "dark dualism" does not (*In Hawthorne's Shadow: American Romance from Melville to Mailer*, 86). Shannon Burns offers the

Gadamer to bear on O'Connor's critique of modern culture, this study moves beyond religious approaches to her fiction by grounding her cultural critique of modernity within the American Romance tradition and the moral dimension fundamental to the genre. The inclusion of Gadamer's philosophical hermeneutics interprets Hawthorne's and O'Connor's critique of the rationalism that underlies modern notions of progress as the scientism of modern method. This study asserts the truth claims of aesthetic experience against the claims to objectivity of scientific knowledge that Hawthorne and O'Connor demonstrate as destructive in their fiction. As he chooses romance over realism, Hawthorne calls into question the fundamental dualism of modernity. O'Connor will revise Hawthorne's formulation of the romance in order to meet the demands of her own artistic vision and Christian belief.

---

observation that the "neutral territory" established by the romance tradition suggests the mystery and ambiguity of life, generally. Because her interest is primarily in this plurality of meaning, Burns argues that O'Connor is more properly to be understood as a writer of romance than as a Christian writer ("The Literary Theory of Flannery O'Connor and Nathaniel Hawthorne"). Finally, Marion Montgomery makes explicit thematic connections between Hawthorne and O'Connor in his well-known trilogy and study of gnosticism, entitled *The Prophetic Poetic and the Spirit of the Age*, the first and third volumes of which are devoted to O'Connor and Hawthorne, respectively.

1

## OUTSIDE OBSERVERS:
## HAWTHORNE'S ARTISTS AND IDEALISTS

In his Preface to *The House of the Seven Gables*, Nathaniel
Hawthorne defines the romance as literary mode. He differentiates
the romance from the novel in terms of the freedom it offers the
writer in the representation of reality. He explains that while the
realism of the novel presumes a careful fidelity to the probable, to
the details of ordinary experience, the writer of romance is free,
according to the laws of convention, to present reality as it is conceived in the mind. She conveys the "truth ... under circumstances"
of her "own choosing and creation" (vii). The creative mind of the
romance writer thus conceives a "neutral territory,"[1] a reality not to
be known objectively, as it always involves this element of
subjectivity, or the blending of the inner and outer worlds. Through
his choice of mimetic mode, Hawthorne undermines the rationalism
of the modern era—the subject/object dichotomy upon which
scientific certainty is based. His traditionally romantic settings evoke
distant times and places; he brings the past to bear on the present,
fiction on fact, as he corroborates the "truth" of his narratives with
fireside legend, or finds the source of his major romance hidden in
an attic, entombed in dust. For readers of Hawthorne, knowledge
seems to come to us, as it does to his protagonists, in his tales of
initiation, from within a "twilight" region that obscures clear vision,
or suggests a limited perceptual horizon. His romances suggest a

---

[1] Nathaniel Hawthorne, "The Custom House," in *The Scarlet Letter* in
vol. 1, *The Centenary Edition of the Works of Nathaniel Hawthorne*
(Columbus: Ohio State University Press, 1962) 36.

condition of limited knowledge in which subject is not easily separated from object, knower from known. To assume a standpoint outside of, or transcendent to, this limited horizon implies the disruptive dualisms that underlie the dramatic conflicts of his fiction. Hawthorne's scientists, his idealist philosophers, Puritans, and to some extent his artists, all suffer from a dichotomizing worldview that objectifies the world outside themselves, that lifts them above the "magnetic chain of humanity,"[2] and thereby disintegrates human community.

Hawthorne's critique of the dichotomous vision that his choice of genre implies begins at home. Living in Concord and writing in the mid-nineteenth century, Hawthorne shared some of the views of his Transcendentalist compeers, particularly those grounded in their common Romantic heritage. Like Emerson and Thoreau, he privileges the imagination over the rationalism that dominated the preceding two centuries. As Hester's embroidered letter "A" suggests, his works celebrate the creative impulse of the artist and individual and the democratic impulse by means of which they make their visions of beauty and truth accessible. Where he differs from the Transcendentalists and other Romantics is in their belief in the inherent goodness of human nature, untouched by the corrupting influence of civilization, and therefore in the perfectibility of humankind. Fundamental to this Romantic belief in progress, and equally disagreeable to Hawthorne, is the Transcendentalist belief in the transparency between the self and the other, the ultimate knowability or intelligibility of the object, which places the human subject at the center of creation.

In his premier essay, "Nature," Emerson outlines the principles of his American Transcendentalist philosophy.[3] He divides the

---

[2] ———, "Ethan Brand," in *The Snow Image and Uncollected Tales* in vol. 11, *The Centenary Edition of the Works of Nathaniel Hawthorne* (Columbus: Ohio State University Press, 1974) 99.

[3] Ralph Waldo Emerson, "Nature," in *Five Essays on Man and Nature*, ed. Robert E. Spiller (New York: Harlan, 1957).

universe into "Nature" and "Soul," the self and the "Not-me" (2), and explains the process by which reconciliation is not only possible, but is already manifest. He describes an "Over-Soul" infusing creation, a universal essence existing in the human mind as "Reason" and in the natural world as "Spirit," forming a correspondence between the mind and external reality (13). For Emerson, then, nature is a reflection of consciousness and, therefore, has moral significance. This is seen mostly clearly in his description of nature as the origin of language. Words reflect appearances in the natural world, which in turn symbolize mental or spiritual states. Nature is therefore emblematic—an outward sign of a spiritual reality, or a reflection of the human mind. The Universal Spirit that informs creation thus forms a unity between humankind and nature, a state of perfection, order, or harmony from which we, as humans, have slipped, living on the edge of our true potential. In his characteristically poetic style, Emerson writes that we live as travelers roasting our eggs over the embers of a volcano (16).

To overcome this discrepancy between our present state and potential, Emerson argues that we must consult the ministry of nature, "unfallen" as it is not subjected to the human will, as well as our own Intuition. The "universe then becomes transparent [to us], and the light of higher laws than its own shines through it" (17). Thus, Emerson places humankind at the center of creation. The natural world, though perfect and inviolable, is "a remoter and inferior incarnation of God, a projection of God in the unconscious" (33); humankind is the point from which all meaning and perspective ultimately emanate. Emerson illustrates this concept with his metaphor of the eye as the "best of artists" (7), composing and producing perspective through the action of its structure as well as "the laws of light." The "landscape becomes round and symmetrical" (7). Emerson thus symbolizes the ideal of unity central to his philosophy with an image of humanity as a "transparent eyeball," reflecting the universal Spirit and creating, molding, or shaping external reality (4). Accordingly, then, as Emerson begins his essay by exhorting his fellow Americans to cast off tradition in order to build "an original relation to the universe," he makes explicit his assumptions of power and possibility regarding our relation to the natural world. "Nature is thoroughly mediate," he writes; it is "made to serve" and ultimately reducible to the "double" of human will (20).

This same relation between the self and nature, though tempered by his sense of the mystery of nature, informs the work of Thoreau, Emerson's friend and student.[4] His retreat to Walden Pond, building his house of the simplest and purest materials found there, suggests a Transcendentalist confidence in the reconstruction of the self. Similarly, in his essay "Walking,"[5] he urges the reader to walk outside the bounds of the village in order to seek the "springs of life" (596), the raw substance of life found in the woods, meadows, and swamps. Pointing explicitly to the Romantic correlation between the self and nature, he explains that there are as many perspectives offered by the surrounding landscape within an afternoon's walk as there are in "threescore years and ten of human life" (598). Thoreau further explains that his direction is always West, placing this metaphorical journey into the self within its American cultural, historical context of progressive movement or westward expansion. The West, as represented by the American frontier, or the New World is always a place from which to start over, free from the Old World and its institutions. Therefore, like Emerson, Thoreau points to the symbolic value of natural fact in this forward-looking essay as he equates the grandeur of the American landscape with the potentiality of the self; the intellect, heart, and soul of the American

---

[4] Thoreau's *The Maine Woods* differs quite radically from the Transcendentalist idealism presented in *Walden* and in such essays as *"Walking,"* especially in his account of the barren and tangled wilderness atop Mount Ktaadn.

[5] Henry David Thoreau, "Walking," in *The Essays of Henry D. Thoreau*, ed. Lewis Hyde (New York: Northpoint, 2002).

people will be commensurate with the height of the American trees, the depth of the great lakes, and the freshness and clarity of the sky.

As stated above, Hawthorne's difference with the Transcendentalists regarding human progress rests on his beliefs regarding the nature of human nature. This difference is particularly clear in his sketch, "Earth's Holocaust," in which he examines the ideal of progress and Emerson's doctrine of self-reliance in order to make his own contrasting beliefs explicit.[6] The sketch is set in the West on a "boundless plain," where a bonfire has been kindled to rid the world of its "worn-out trumpery" (381). The reformers begin by casting into the flames such trivial items as old newspapers and magazines. By beginning with this small act of destruction, Hawthorne intimates that Thoreau may have been right in *Walden* in considering these things as expendable, containing merely gossip, and no essential or eternal truths. Similarly, Hawthorne seems to condone the destruction of "rubbish" from the herald's office, as medals and ribbons from various monarchies are thrown into the fire, signifying the triumph, hard earned and once and for all, of the revolutionary spirit. The voice of his narrator's wise guide, however, playing here the role of Dante's Virgil, wonders what "worse nonsense" (384) may replace this admittedly outdated form of government. Various popular reform movements of Hawthorne's day then provide their own combustibles for the fire. Zealots of the temperance movement destroy all the liquor of the world, mixing, as the obviously cultivated narrator notes, the most precious wines from some of the finest vintages into one stream with the vile liquids of the "common pot-house." Confident that they have at last delivered the world from the "curse of ages," the reformers rejoice as the intoxicants send a spire of flame arching against the firmament, threatening "to set the sky itself on fire" (386). Similarly, coffees, teas, and tobaccos are tossed onto the "heap of inutility and set ablaze" (387). Onlookers,

---

[6] Nathaniel Hawthorne, "Earth's Holocaust," in *Mosses from an Old Manse* in vol. 10, *The Centenary Edition of the Works of Nathaniel Hawthorne* (Columbus: Ohio State University Press, 1974).

attempting to rid themselves of reminders of life's disappointments and shortcomings, throw personal effects into the fire. A widow, intent on a second marriage, discards a picture of her late husband; a frustrated author throws away his pen and paper; a depressed and half-crazed woman, convinced of her own worthlessness, attempts to throw herself into the public fire of reform. Others throw away marriage certificates, title deeds, notes of debt and credit. As the narrator continues, he reports that the spirit of reform, based in confidence that the reign of reason will bring about universal peace, causes the crowd to bring all the world's munitions and arms of war, as well as the instruments of capital punishment, to the fire. In an increasingly ironic tone, he notes that this same belief in progress motivates the destruction of libraries, of old classics that Hawthorne's "modern philosophers" believe to press too heavily on the "living intellect" (395). Finally, this confidence in the forward march of humanity leads the zealous reformers to their most significant and potentially dangerous reform. As the narrator looks on in astonishment and consternation, the reformers "consummate this great Act of Faith" by heaping onto the blaze all sacred emblems, popish, Protestant, and Puritan (399). Though he at first remembers the reassurances offered by his Transcendentalist primer, that only the temporal, cultural superfluities of religion are being destroyed here, and nothing essential—"the wood-paths" are after all "the aisles of our cathedral," the "firmament … its ceiling"—he soon wonders at the rashness of their act, the all-consuming ardency of their fire of reform (400). Having at first thrown away only the outmoded trappings of a derelict form of government and various other used-up, worn-out, and luxury items, the "Titan of innovation" has now laid hold of the very pillars of our cultural heritage, grasping at and leveling "every human or divine appendage of our mortal state" (401). The narrator ironically declares that "truths, which the Heavens trembled at, were now but a fable of the world's infancy"; the human race "had grown too enlightened to define their faith within a form of words" or to "limit the spiritual by any analogy to" the material (400). The moral meaning of Hawthorne's sketch is made clear, however, when his wise guide informs him that such is actually not the case; any valuable truth that he may seek will have survived the conflagration. Indeed the Holy Book is seen to be upon the heap, its pages—having been purified of human fingerprints and marginalia—assuming a more brilliant whiteness. Hawthorne ends the sketch with a passage that, as Hyatt Waggoner has rightly asserted, may serve as a key to all of his work.[7] In a conversation that takes place around the dying embers of the fire, a "dark-complexioned personage" reassures the Last Thief, the Last Murderer, the Last Toper, and the hangman that the "old world," the world of sin, folly, limitation and liability, will surely return, as the reformers have neglected to throw the human heart into the fire. "And, unless they hit upon some method of purifying that foul cavern," he explains, "forth from it will re-issue all the shapes of wrong and misery ... which they have taken such a vast deal of trouble to consume to ashes." The human heart, Hawthorne's narrator concludes, is a "boundless sphere" that confounds and eludes our age-long efforts at reform as it constitutes an "error at the very root of the matter!" (403). The erring human heart forms an essential aspect of our humanity.

This sketch thus demonstrates Hawthorne's skepticism regarding the Transcendentalist ideal of progress as it is based in the belief in the perfectibility of human nature. Experience and human history suggested to Hawthorne that the human heart was indeed a "boundless sphere," divided and unknowable, and, therefore, not to be included within the category of natural phenomena over which the scientific and progressive sensibility was asserting dominion. Therefore, Emerson's idealism, which did not adequately account for the reality of evil as Hawthorne represents it, rang hollow. Hawthorne's fiction suggests that placing humankind at the center of creation, as Emerson does, results in a subjectivism that ultimately

---

[7] Hyatt H. Waggoner, *Hawthorne: A Critical Study*, rev. ed. (Cambridge MA: Belknap-Harvard University Press, 1963) 22.

reduces the world to an object for human utility.[8] Hawthorne, therefore, concerns himself much more frequently with the danger of pride in his characterizations, than with the virtues of self-reliance.[9] Against the liberal ideals of progress and perfectibility, Hawthorne asserts "the truth of the human heart," the realities of death, sin, and suffering. Given the limitations he imposes on human reason, he thus asserts the finiteness of being as well as knowing, an ontological and epistemological condition of finitude, dramatized by the genre of romance.

Hawthorne's notion of romance, then, as he defines it in his fiction, does not suggest the ideal reconciliation between art and nature, or the pastoral impulse that runs throughout American letters and motivates much of American Transcendentalist thought.[10] Indeed, the self-contained harmony of Hawthorne's pastoral retreat is shattered, as he reports it in a notebook entry of July 1844, as the shriek of a locomotive bursts in upon it; the scattered clouds

---

[8] A notorious example of the subjectivism at the heart of Emerson's Transcendentalism can be found in a passage regarding the value of nature as a source of "Discipline" in his essay "Nature." Emerson writes: "Nature is thoroughly mediate. It is made to serve. It receives the dominion of man as meekly as the ass on which the Savior rode. It offers all its kingdoms to man as the raw material which he may mold into what is useful. Man is never weary of working it up …. One after another his victorious thought comes up with and reduces all things, until the world becomes at last only a realized will—the double of the man" ("Nature," 20).

[9] Waggoner, *Hawthorne: A Critical Study*, 16.

[10] I refer to Leo Marx's definition of the pastoral ideal in *The Machine in the Garden*. Marx reiterates the traditional observation that the motive of the good shepherd of the Virgilian pastoral mode was not simply to escape from city to wilderness, but to search for balance between the opposed worlds of town and country, mind and world, art and nature. It was an ideal reconciliation that, in Marx's reading, has been used to underscore Utopian dreams of America as "New World," since the Age of Discovery. Such an ideal, Marx argues, has become a dominant symbol in American culture and imagination and a characteristic motif in American literature (*The Machine in the Garden: Technology and the Pastoral Ideal in America*).

overhead signal the ruin of a "dreamer's Utopia."[11] Thus, Thoreau's hut at Walden, which, as metaphor for the mind, he assures us, can be reconstructed, autonomously, anywhere and everywhere (125), is countered in Hawthorne's fiction by his image of "the house of the seven gables." The house, the legendary mansion of the Pyncheon family, is built on the bones of Matthew Maule, the original owner, who is wrongly executed for witchcraft. Colonel Pyncheon, the zealous and acquisitive Puritan who seeks to gain possession of his land, joins vehemently in the general outcry against Maule. From the outset, then, the land upon which the house is built carries the curse of this wrongful death, and other crimes committed in relation to it, throughout the ages. The ownership of the house is thus marked by an act of "original sin" that relates this family to the history of humanity. Hawthorne is explicit in his use of metaphor that identifies the house with the Pyncheon family, and, by extension, with what he believes to be the history of human experience. "The aspect of the venerable mansion," he writes, has always impressed him as a "human countenance." Its once stately and magnificent architecture is in a state of ruin, manifesting in its outward expression the "long lapse of mortal life" and the vicissitudes of fortune "that have passed within" (5). The portrait of the original Pyncheon owner still hangs in the room in which he died—coincidentally on his first day of occupation, casting his "stern, immitigable features" over his progeny, like an "Evil Genius" destined to haunt his race (21). The current inhabitant of the house, Hepzibah Pyncheon, is aged, decrepit, and alienated. Wearing a perpetual frown caused by failing eyesight, she is misunderstood by the townspeople, and presents an image both comic and tragic for the reader. Like the ruined house she inhabits, Hepzibah bears the marks of her lineage and the burden of history upon her. Similarly, her heart, although worn and tattered, reveals—like tufts of verdant moss within the crevices of the

---

[11] Nathaniel Hawthorne, *The American Notebooks* in vol. 8, *The Centenary Edition of the Works of Nathaniel Hawthorne* (Columbus: Ohio State University Press, 1972) 250.

mansion's gables—an unfailing commitment to care for her invalid brother Clifford, who has been wrongly imprisoned for thirty years. There is, then, within Hawthorne's human habitation, burdened as it is with guilt, death, and decay, the possibility for renewal and regeneration—though not easily or ideally given, as Transcendentalist philosophy would suggest.

In *The Blithedale Romance*, Hawthorne's most explicitly pastoral romance, he satirizes the utopian impulse that runs counter to this image of our human nature set forth metaphorically by his "house of the seven gables." [12] The story is a fictional treatment of the Brooks Farm experiment in communal living in which Hawthorne himself took part for a short time. The actual experiment failed, and Hawthorne's representation reveals his speculations as to why. The cast of characters includes Zenobia, a self-reliant and queenly reformer, and author of feminist political tracts; Priscilla, an angelic and somewhat ineffectual maiden along the lines of Phoebe in *The House of the Seven Gables* and Hilda in *The Marble Faun*; Miles Coverdale, a minor poet well read in Transcendentalism; and Hollingsworth, a compassionate, though monomaniacal, philanthropist. The story opens as the narrator, Miles Coverdale, quits his comfortable apartments and ventures forth into a blinding snowstorm in order to embark upon his quest for a better life at the Blithedale

---

[12] ————, *The Blithedale Romance and Fanshawe* in vol. 3, *The Centenary Edition of the Works of Nathaniel Hawthorne* (Columbus: Ohio State University Press, 1964). Critics have remarked that Hawthorne's parody of the liberal idealism of the Blithedalers makes this tale an "antipastoral." Richard Chase notes that Hawthorne's portrayal of the "civilized utopians" set against the innocence of their natural backdrop makes Hawthorne "a partisan of conventional society as he finds it" (*The American Novel and Its Tradition*, 85). Similarly, Robert Fogle points out that the pastoral retreat enables the Blithedalers to embark on behaviors that are alien to "conventional society." He notes Coverdale's observation regarding the retreat that "While inclining us to the soft affections of the golden age, it seemed to authorize any individual, of either sex, to fall in love with any other, regardless of what would elsewhere be judged suitable and prudent" (*Hawthorne's Fiction: The Light and the Dark*, 143).

community (10). He joins the other utopianists who have similarly escaped the constraints of city life, and have come to Blithedale to begin their experiment, the moral end of which they believe to be the reformation of the world. From the beginning, then, the tone of mock heroism with which Coverdale narrates events undercuts the validity of the whole affair with irony, while a more somber tone and images point directly to Hawthorne's own lack of confidence in the enterprise. Employing an image that equates the human heart and hearth, he opens the second chapter with a reminiscence of the huge country kitchen fire that warmed the community members gathered around it on the first day. The narrator, now wearied by age and experience, describes the once commodious fire: "The staunch oaken-logs were long ago burnt out. Their genial glow must be represented, if at all, by the merest phosphoric glimmer, like that which exudes, rather than shines, from damp fragments of decayed trees, deluding the benighted wanderer through a forest" (9).

"Around such chill mockery of a fire," the communitarians had sat, spreading their palms toward its "imaginary warmth," talking over their "exploded scheme" for "beginning the life of Paradise anew" (9). Hawthorne adds to the irony of their present situation by noting that the strength of this hearth fire on the first evening at Blithedale was assisted by brushwood, known for its quick combustibility and short-lived brilliancy. Similarly, its blaze, which illuminates the windows against the blowing snowstorm, is still hardly sufficient to fend off the dark, "undefined," and desolate space that presses in on the reformers. Through this equation of images, then, Hawthorne undermines the viability of the reformers' experiment as it is based on the durability of their feelings of good will and beneficence toward one another. Other images as well bode the possible failure of their humanistic project and call into question the sincerity of their motives. Zenobia is identified with an exotic greenhouse flower that characteristically adorns her hair. She gently mocks Coverdale for suggesting that they leave off cooking and gather their food, mid-winter, from some Edenic bounty he presumes to be there. This image of the artificial flower is augmented by a theater metaphor that Hawthorne introduces in his Preface that suggests that indeed something insubstantial may be at the heart of their enterprise. He describes his fictional representation of Brook Farm as a "theater," where his characters could play their "phantasmagorical antics" (1). While Hawthorne is no doubt engaging here in his characteristic self-deprecation regarding the substance of his romance genre, his characters do often exhibit a lack of earnestness regarding their participation in the project, assuming attitudes that more befit spectators. The characters thus play at charades; they "play" at, or make a game of, naming their community, in turn considering as possibilities "Utopia," "The Oasis"—or "Sahara" in case of failure—and finally settling on "Blithedale"—the happy valley. Finally, both Coverdale and Zenobia refer to their own "mock-life" (227) at Blithedale as "an illusion, a masquerade, a pastoral" (21). The play, of course, ends tragically as Zenobia, betrayed by Hollingsworth, drowns herself in despair. The life of the "knot of dreamers," as Hawthorne describes them in the title to chapter three, thus ends, and the forward thinking community is dissolved.

The characterization of Miles Coverdale as artist and player points to a character type prevalent throughout Hawthorne's fiction. He is a remote, cool observer, ethically uncommitted, and offering no deep emotional response to the events in the lives of the people who surround him.[13] He watches as the scenes of the drama unfold

---

[13] Hawthorne's treatment of the artist figure invites a wide range of critical speculation. While such stories as "The Artist of the Beautiful" and "The Snow Image" point, even if ambiguously, to the priority of the imagination over the utilitarian spirit of the nineteenth century, critical consensus is that Hawthorne's artists, generally, embody the cool, objectifying reserve characteristic of the head/heart dichotomy. My argument in reading Hawthorne's artists in the light of contemporary hermeneutics is that such a tendency to objectify an other can be read as a tendency to "aestheticize" experience, to commit an act of abstraction against a person or an object that is characteristic of the subjectivism of modern method. Our understanding of

before him, as his fellow members of this utopian community fall victim to their own natures. Zenobia, proud, intelligent, and willful, falls in love with the sexist Hollingsworth, who is willing to take her money to finance his projects of reform, but casts her aside in order to accept the unfettered adulation of Priscilla. As spectator of this tragedy involving his three companions, he offers himself up to the reader as the Greek chorus, providing analysis in terms of meaning and moral and aesthetic judgment on the scenes before him (97). Thus, as his name implies, Coverdale continually seeks "cover," safe seclusion from which he may peep and eavesdrop on the community members of Blithedale. He climbs into his treetop "hermitage" (an activity significant enough to warrant a chapter title) and spies on Zenobia and Hollingsworth. From this remote location, he eavesdrops as well on an interview between her and Westervelt, Hawthorne's devil figure in this tale, and someone Coverdale knows to be mysteriously entangled in her past and possibly intent on doing her harm. He is aware of this speculative tendency that causes him to pry with disinterested curiosity into the passions of others and fears that it has "gone far toward unhumanizing his heart" (154). Still, he continues to "linger on the brink," and in his role as minor poet, turns the tragedy of Blithedale into a ballad, which, as Zenobia no doubt correctly fears, will soften the moral she imparts to him before her death, when finally he writes the poem down.[14] The tale ends, then,

---

the tragic consequences of the head/heart dualism in Hawthorne's fiction can thus take on added significance when seen within the context of Gadamer's critique of modern scientific method as the ruling paradigm for achieving knowledge.

[14] Critics point out that Hawthorne's singular use of a first-person narrator in *The Blithedale Romance* may mitigate the charge of detachment leveled against so many of Hawthorne's artist/idealists. Fogle argues that in this novel Hawthorne balances his traditionally objective and balanced point of view with that of the subjective perspective of a first person narrator. This use of point of view is complicated by the fact that Hawthorne gives Coverdale a large part in the story. Since Hawthorne chooses to place his narrator in the forefront, Coverdale "is forced to maintain a delicate balance between spectator and participant which must not be upset" (156). Terence Martin

after the death of Zenobia and the dissolution of the community, with Coverdale's admission that there is nothing to tell of himself; he has made but a "dim" figure in his own narrative, taking whatever color his own life has from the "hue" of the lives of those surrounding him (245).

Hawthorne's critique of the lack of empathy characteristic of Coverdale finds a correlation in Gadamer's notion of the aesthetic sensibility that he develops in his critique of modern scientific method. Gadamer's critique of method rests on its separation of subject and object in its pursuit of its ideal of objective knowledge. The subject, or person seeking knowledge, removes himself from history, from personal prejudice, in order to come to know an object in itself, or objectively. In his argument against modern methodology, Gadamer describes the achievement of knowledge as rather a "fusion of horizons," [15] in which parties to a dialogue come together in mutual understanding. He here distinguishes between the engaged, empathetic sensibility that recognizes knowledge to be the result of experience, or the product of an encounter, and what he calls an "aesthetic consciousness." Basing his analysis of all understanding on that achieved in aesthetic experience, or in our

---

sees similar problems in the characterization of Coverdale as he compares him to the narrators of some of Hawthorne's earlier tales and sketches. While Coverdale is drawn to meet the conventions of these earlier and lesser pieces, Martin argues, he differs from them in that he evolves into a character in his own right. As he wishes to become involved in the world around him, Martin writes, he is "released into a world which has no real need of him" (*Nathaniel Hawthorne,* 148). He ultimately comes to find himself "in search of a role" (154). Chase insightfully relates problems with Coverdale as narrator to Hawthorne's own problems as writer. He observes that Coverdale's ambivalence regarding his involvement with the lives of his friends is reflected in Hawthorne's scruples regarding the role of novelist. The detached role of the novelist, Chase writes, caused Hawthorne himself to fear that he would commit the Unpardonable Sin. He thus chooses the role of romancer rather than "to take [his] place among the great novelists" (*The American Novel*, 87).

[15] Gadamer, *Truth and Method*, 273.

encounter with a work of art, he explains that, with the priority given rationalism by modern science, aesthetic being and aesthetic experience become "merely" aesthetic. That is, because human reason, assisted by scientific method, could come to know objects positively, in themselves, art came to be seen as imitation, representation, or appearance, divorced ontologically from its object, the original, and, therefore, contributing no real, substantive knowledge to our understanding of the world. The experience of art thus fell victim to an aestheticizing, or "aesthetic," consciousness that, drawing a sharp distinction between art and reality, removed the artwork from its real relation to the world, depriving it of its meaning. The work of art, thus emptied of content, becomes the object of the aesthetic consciousness, which, denying the relation of the work to its world and consequently to itself, likewise reduces the aesthetic experience to disinterested pleasure in the purely aesthetic, in style, or form. Gadamer argues that this same process of abstraction, which seeks to know an object in itself, characterizes the scientific mode of knowing, generally. In the nineteenth-century hermeneutics of Schleiermacher and Dilthey, for instance, Gadamer explains that understanding was achieved by means of the "divinatory act." A person correctly understands when he is able to transform himself into an other or "divine" the mind of another in order to capture an original intention of meaning (261). In any case of possible understanding, Gadamer explains, to come to know an object in itself means that we must isolate it within history, thereby reducing it, and ultimately gaining dominion over it, as the "understanding" consciousness (270). Thus, the character of Coverdale, in Hawthorne's romance, would represent this aesthetic consciousness as he seeks to "identify" his mind with that of Old Moodie (84) in order to satisfy his spectator's curiosity regarding the obviously painful details of the old man's past. Coverdale similarly warns, only half seriously, of the damaging consequences of this placing of one's friends under a microscope for examination, pulling them apart and piecing them back together again. The purpose of his experiment is foiled; he laments that the fragmented whole yields unsatisfactory results regarding knowledge of the true nature of their being.

In contrast to Coverdale, in his characterization of Hollingsworth Hawthorne points more sharply and without humor to the ethical consequences of the aesthetic sensibility. As a philanthropist and nineteenth-century reformer, Hollingsworth holds progressive ideals that most accurately represent those of the utopian community, though he does not share in the particular aims of Blithedale. He is described by Coverdale to be a man of great heart, generosity, and benevolence, whose dedication to his ideal ultimately corrupts him and destroys his humanity. Channeling his energy and passion toward his ideal, Hollingsworth is ultimately "incorporated" by it, as Coverdale explains; the fulfillment of this one end becomes his own fulfillment. His "godlike benevolence" is thus debased into an "all-devouring egotism," for which he is willing to sacrifice all of his human attachments, his love for others as well as their love for him (71). As Hawthorne characterizes him, Hollingsworth is thus guilty of a great act of abstraction; he loves humankind, but ceases to love human beings. When he can no longer utilize them for the attainment of his goal, as his treatment of Coverdale and Zenobia attests, he discards them as he would a "broken tool" (218). Hollingsworth's character, therefore, epitomizes the imbalance of head and heart that, with varying degrees of severity in its impact on human community, runs throughout Hawthorne's fiction. As Hollingsworth's heart is corrupted by theory, the outcome of the Blithedale adventure demonstrates Hawthorne's critique of the doctrine of natural goodness held dear by the social engineers of the nineteenth century, and the spiritual and intellectual pride that may obscure their vision.

Perhaps the consummate example of the pride and naïvete that underlies the efforts of the idealist reformer is Holgrave in *The House of the Seven Gables*. Introduced as an artist—a daguerreotypist—he is guilty of the same tendency toward abstraction, though to a lesser degree, as Coverdale. Renting a room in one of the gables, Holgrave remains the aloof observer, closely attentive to the affairs and "individualities" of Hepzibah and Clifford, but seeming to be more in "quest of mental food" than to be affected by any human, that is, compassionate or empathetic, response or desire to help them (177–78). As Phoebe charges, he looks upon the house as if it were a theater, and upon Hepzibah's and Clifford's misfortunes as if they were tragedy (217). Indeed, he admits that, in regards to the pair, he suspects that "Destiny is arranging its fifth act for catastrophe" (218). His characteristic disinterestedness is further underscored by the description of him as "homeless" and uncommitted. He is the "wandering daguerreotypist" (244), who has picked up his current trade of photography as easily as the many other occupations by which he has earned his living. He is thus marked, for Phoebe, by a "lack of reverence for what was fixed, unless, at a moment's warning, it could establish its right to hold its ground" (177). In a conversation with Phoebe, his characteristic vagrancy takes the form of Emerson's doctrine of American self-reliance:

> Shall we never, never get rid of this Past? ... It lies upon the Present like a giant's dead body .... We read in Dead Men's books! We laugh at Dead Men's jokes, and cry at Dead Men's pathos .... We worship the living Deity according to Dead Men's forms and creeds! ... I ought to have said, too, that we live in Dead Men's houses; as, for instance, in this of the Seven Gables! (182–83)

Here Holgrave clearly serves Hawthorne as a spokesperson for the liberal ideals of nineteenth-century America. He is characterized by a youthfulness and optimism that is enriching and life-enhancing in its creativity (an energy that Hawthorne claims "a mature man had better die at once than ... utterly relinquish" [179]), but that may be rash and destructive, and too idealistic, or unrealistic, in its method.[16]

---

[16] As critics note, Hawthorne's appraisal of Holgrave is, to a great extent, favorable. Martin notes his role as gardener, as he tends the Pyncheon

In his enthusiasm for reform, he seeks to level in order to rebuild, denying history, and equating the past with death. "Just think a moment," Holgrave continues, "and it will startle you to see what slaves we are to bygone times—to Death, if we give the matter the right word!" (183). Giving voice, then, to Hawthorne's metaphor that links house to humanity, he scorns the house of the seven gables as the most appalling example of the burden of history on the human spirit, of the remorse, "discontent and anguish," that have lived within the walls of the Pyncheon ancestral home. Such a "house," he proclaims, as figure for the tainted blood of our human lineage, must be "purified with fire" until "only its ashes remain" (184).

---

garden, systematically pulling the weeds and fostering growth. His fault, as the images of his rootlessness make clear, lies in the radical nature of his belief that the past can be completely eradicated, that the house of the seven gables can be razed as an example of the "odious and abominable Past" (*Seven Gables,* 184). Martin thus reads the ending of the tale, Holgrave's capitulation of his radical beliefs and acceptance of more conservative ones, as a compromise that demonstrates Hawthorne's values. The past must be balanced with the present. Nina Baym, on the other hand, credits Hawthorne's portrayal of Holgrave as a youthful reformer, but is sorely disappointed in the ending of the novel. Holgrave's marriage to Phoebe and move to the country estate mark no improvement in the relations between man and woman. Having surrendered his radical opinions, he now looks to Phoebe only for comfort, rather than creativity, and their move is complete with "dependents" ("Hawthorne's Holgrave: The Failure of the Artist-Hero" in *Critical Essays on Hawthorne's* The House of the Seven Gables, 71). Fogle, similar to Martin, argues that the final marriage of Holgrave and Phoebe provides a balance of the head and heart that seems consistent with Hawthorne's subject of the "truth of the human heart." "Boundless and divided," it is unknowable, and its errors are not susceptible to the ideals of the reformer, any more than Holgrave's daguerreotypes, though aided by the clear light of the sun, can capture the whole picture, or any better than Giovanni can apprehend the complexity of a moral situation in his understanding of Beatrice. This latter point is made in contrast to Baym's observation that Holgrave's portraits—aided by sunlight—reflect the truth of Judge Pyncheon's character. It doesn't seem likely to me that the "clear light" of day, in this instance, can assist moral vision any better than it does anywhere else in Hawthorne's fiction.

This desire to be "unhoused," to transcend history, or ease the burden of time and the imposition of matter, is echoed by Clifford in the chapter that describes his flight, with Hepzibah, from the house of the seven gables. He attempts to escape, by rail, from his past, from the wrongs done him by Jaffrey Pyncheon, and from the house itself as the scene of his despair and the visible manifestation of the Pyncheon lineage. Like Holgrave, he considers the house, as symbol for human history, to be like an ill-fitting garment, or skin, that can be cast off. Described not as an artist, but as a lover of the beautiful, Clifford is a character that Hawthorne does not take too seriously. He is portrayed as someone of overwrought sensitivity and sentimentality who speaks of a linear progression of history in which the "coarse and the sensual" will eventually be refined away. Technological advancement will eliminate the evil that gathers around the hearth. He, therefore, declares that locomotives, which "spiritualize travel" and "annihilate the toil and dust of pilgrimage," will restore us to our original nomadic existence, when, unfettered by our prisons of brick, stone, and mortar, we will regain our freedom and power (260). Clifford thus envisions a time, as did Emerson, when technology will effect a sort of pastoral peace, when the mind will no longer have to yield to matter, and the realities of human history, of being "housed," or "embodied," will no longer stand in the way of human progress and happiness.[17] He offers the example of electricity as support for his utopian vision of the future, which rests on philosophical idealism:

Then there is electricity—the demon, the angel, the mighty physical power, the all-pervading intelligence … by means of electricity, the world of matter has become a great nerve ….

---

[17] As Marx points out, Emerson promoted industrial and technological innovation as a means by which to achieve the pastoral ideal in America. Industrialization would ease the burden of physical labor and even facilitate harmony with the natural world, as we would enlist its resources in the cause of human advancement. This is, of course, evident in Emerson's discussion of nature as "commodity" in his essay, "Nature."

Rather, the round globe is a vast head, a brain, instinct with intelligence! Or, shall we say, it is itself a thought; nothing but thought, and no longer the substance which we deemed it. (264)

Among Hawthorne's reformers, such idealism, as we have seen, turns quickly to a subjectivism that encroaches on the world around it.[18] The zealous desire to improve humankind rests ultimately on the ability to separate mind from matter, subject from object. As such, the sensibility of the reformer is necessarily nomadic; it transcends its own history, eschews all ties to time and place, in order to occupy, and hence to know and be able to control, its object. The human heart thus becomes an object of investigation much like the natural phenomena under the study of the scientist who, assisted by method, seeks knowledge for domination.

The tragic potential for misuse of the modern scientific attitude is the subject of "Rappaccini's Daughter."[19] Here, the idealistic vision of young Giovanni takes the life of the young and beautiful Beatrice. The story is set in a garden, created by the renowned physician Rappaccini. From his rented quarters in Rappaccini's mansion, Giovanni Guasconti, a young medical student, observes the garden and describes what he sees. At its

---

[18] As Martin notes, Clifford's idealism and portrayal as a dreamer may well have made him an Aylmer, rather than an Owen Warland. To this end, Martin observes Hawthorne's comment regarding the possibility for perversion of the creative impulse within Clifford and the effect of his long incarceration in deterring it. Hawthorne writes that had Clifford possessed the means of cultivating his taste for beauty "to its utmost perfectibility" in his earlier life, "that subtle attribute might, before this period, have completely eaten out or filed away his affections. Shall we venture to pronounce, therefore, that his long and black calamity may not have had a redeeming drop of mercy at the bottom?" (qtd. in Martin, *Nathaniel Hawthorne,* 135).

[19] Nathaniel Hawthorne, "Rappaccini's Daughter," in *Mosses from an Old Manse* in vol. 10, *The Centenary Edition of the Works of Nathaniel Hawthorne* (Columbus: Ohio State University Press, 1974).

center, and likewise central to the thematic significance of the story, are the ruined remains of a marble fountain, "sculptured with rare art," Guasconti explains, "but so woefully shattered that it was impossible to trace the original design from the … remaining fragments." The water from the fountain, however, "continued to gush and sparkle into the sunbeams as cheerfully as ever" (94). The image of the garden and its shattered fountain thus points once again to what Hawthorne believes to be the real nature of humanity and consequently to his judgment regarding any ideal or Transcendentalist reconciliation between the human self, society, and nature. As he has dramatized it in *The House of the Seven Gables*, our human nature is capable of both good and evil. Though we may have at our base a wellspring of good, the record of sin and suffering that constitutes human history suggests that any redemption or regeneration we may gain will not be achieved by the abstractions of intellect. Thus, though the young and naïve Giovanni at first congratulates himself that "in the heart of the barren city," he had found such luxuriant vegetation to serve as "symbolic language … to keep him in communion with Nature" (98), he soon realizes that Rappaccini, the "scientific gardener," tends his plants with an air of distrust inappropriate to this "most simple and innocent of human toils." He wonders if this garden is the "Eden of the present world … and this man with such a perception of harm in what his own hands caused to grow … the Adam" (95–96).

As the story progresses, the reader discovers, with Giovanni, that the garden is made up of poisonous plants, with whom Beatrice, the beautiful daughter of Rappaccini, shares an intimate communion. Reared with them since infancy, Beatrice explains to Giovanni that while she is merely the earthly child of her scientist father, the plants, particularly the shrub of opulent and gem-like purple blossoms at the center of the fountain, are the offspring "of his science" (123). This peculiar sisterhood between plant and girl is enhanced by Beatrice's physical appearance. Describing her as luxuriously beautiful, full of life and health, Giovanni notes that she heightens the analogy to her sister shrub by both "the arrangement of her dress" and its color (102). In his own narrative voice, however, Hawthorne is careful to point out that though she shares the physical appearance of the plants, she does not share their nature. "Her spirit gushe[s] up before [Giovanni] like a fresh rill"; her thoughts, too, come forth "from a deep source ... as if diamonds and rubies sparkled upward among the bubbles of the fountain" (113). Thus, Beatrice, identified physically with the poisonous plants created by her father, is also identified with the image of the fountain, having as her life source a pure and redolent spirit. Her characterization, therefore, extends Hawthorne's garden metaphor; she, too, is beautiful yet broken in her fallen condition, and, taken together, both girl and garden serve Hawthorne as an apt symbol for humanity.

As readers expect, this complex human nature, inherently and potentially good, yet tainted by frailty, confounds the simple-minded and idealist Giovanni. He sees Beatrice alternately as an angel or a fiend, but never as human. He fears that there must be some "monstrosity of soul" (120) that corresponds to the oddities of her physical nature. Though Hawthorne consistently calls the objective validity of Giovanni's perceptions into question, Giovanni believes he has seen a butterfly drop dead at Beatrice's feet. Fresh flowers have wilted in her hand. A lizard has expired from the touch of a drop of dew from her sister plant. As a result of what he thinks he sees, he therefore alternates between blind faith in what he knows to be the essential purity of her nature and fear that she will contaminate him with the man-made malignancy that has been wrought through her system by her father's science. Determined, then, to bring her back within the "limits of ordinary nature" (119), Giovanni gives her the antidote, which destroys all the evil within her and hence destroys her as well. Hawthorne, therefore, concludes: "as poison had been life, so the powerful antidote was death"; corruption had been an essential aspect of her humanity. Thus, "the poor victim of man's ingenuity and of thwarted nature, and of the fatality that attends all such efforts of perverted wisdom perished there, at the feet of her father and Giovanni" (127–28).

The victimization and death of Beatrice, then, dramatize the inadequacy of the idealism of both Rappaccini and Giovanni in terms of addressing the complexity of human nature. Rappaccini—a man made all-powerful by his knowledge of nature—wishes to erase his daughter's humanity. She becomes the crowning achievement of his career—his "pride and triumph" (127). In losing her humanity, however, she becomes monstrous to others and is condemned to a life of alienation; she leads a lonely life and suffers a premature death. Giovanni, for his part, can neither understand her nor offer compassion for her humanness. Though his vision, the objective truth of his perceptions, is consistently called into question by the ironic undertone of Hawthorne's narrative voice, he has full confidence in his ability to ultimately solve the riddle of her existence and to bring the complexity of her being into the "daylight of ... perfect consciousness" (114). In fixating upon the possibility of evil within her nature, Giovanni reveals the stinginess within his own soul, and he consequently breaks her heart and facilitates her death.

"The Birth-mark" is another story in which abstract intellect trumps compassion as the resource needed to care for the vulnerable flesh.[20] In this poignant example, a young wife dies at the hands of a husband, whom she adores. Aylmer, a preeminent eighteenth-century scientist, becomes so obsessed by the tiny hand-shaped birthmark on the cheek of his young bride Georgiana that he must "have it out" at all costs (40). While Hawthorne notes that other suitors had been charmed by the mark, flattering her with the suggestion that it may be the print of a fairy hand upon

---

[20] ———, "The Birth-mark," in *Mosses from an Old Manse* in vol. 10, *The Centenary Edition of the Works of Nathaniel Hawthorne* (Columbus: Ohio State University Press, 1974).

her, Aylmer regards it critically as "the visible mark of earthly imperfection" (37) and resolves to remove it using the methods of his science. Hawthorne underscores Aylmer's zeal in his characterization of him, as he describes the age as one in which recent discoveries into the secrets of nature had so wooed aspiring scientists that it was not uncommon for the "love of science" to rival the "love of woman" (36). In such an age of burgeoning discovery and optimism, Hawthorne concludes that though Aylmer's love for his new wife Georgiana may indeed "prove the stronger of the two … it could only be by intertwining itself with his love of science" (37). Accordingly, Georgiana's birthmark, signifying as it does for Aylmer "the fatal flaw of [her] humanity" (38), becomes, after their marriage, the sign of his own limitation and an obstacle to his professional ambition. He therefore determines to remove it and, secluding her within his laboratory, administers his concoction.

The laboratory in which Aylmer performs his fatal experiment, and indeed his contrast with his assistant Aminadab, point to the philosophical dualism that informs his faith that he can correct Georgiana's nature. Hawthorne contrasts Aylmer, whom he describes as pale, thin, and scholarly in appearance, with his "under-worker" Aminadab described as shaggy, bulky, and begrimed. Aylmer refers to his assistant as a "human machine" or "thou man of clay" (51). Similarly, the laboratory itself, its "severe and homely simplicity … its naked walls and brick pavement," is in sharp contrast to the rich and luxuriant, yet artificial and decadent, boudoir that serves as Aylmer's personal living quarters (50). Images of perverted nature thus enable the apartment to serve as the very type for Aylmer's mind, and the sharp contrast points up the distinction between mind and matter, art and brute nature. Within these walls, hung with gorgeous and flowing tapestry that seems to "shut in the scene from infinite space," Aylmer secludes Georgiana (44) as he concocts the compound of chemicals that will remove the birthmark. Once again, as in "Rappaccini's

Daughter," the antidote proves too strong for her mortal frame, and Georgiana, as Beatrice before her, is sacrificed to an ideal of perfection and loveliness, and to dreams of unearthly power. Hawthorne thus ends his story with the real results of Aylmer's idealism. As an aspiring and ambitious scientist in an age of seeming miracle wrought by science, Aylmer fails to be checked by the limits or "mysteries" that nature imposes —and that he knows in his heart—as he risks Georgiana's life. As Hawthorne indicates in his characterization of him, Aylmer had long recognized that "our great Creative Mother ... permits us indeed to mar, but seldom to mend, and like a jealous patentee, on no account to make" (42). It is unfortunate that Aylmer's understanding of this natural fact does not prevent the death of his wife, nor allow him to recognize the "short-comings of the composite man—the spirit burthened with clay and working with matter" (49). His death-defying abstraction causes not only Georgiana's death but it also prevents the young scientist's participation in marriage itself as a union of spirit and flesh.[21]

In conclusion, it must be noted that this act of abstraction that can cause a man to kill his wife is characterized by Hawthorne in "Ethan Brand" as no less than the "Unpardonable Sin" of the New Testament. Brand, a lime-burner, returns to his kiln in the Berkshires after he has traveled the world in search of the "Sin." Ironically, he reports to Bartram, the present lime-burner, that though he has searched worldwide for the sin, he has, in fact, discovered that it lies within his own breast, as the conception of the idea of the search itself. In this story, as in his pairing of Aylmer and his partner Aminadab, Hawthorne uses the intense physicality of Bartram to underscore the intellectuality and

---

[21] Liz Rosenberg makes the wonderful point that not only is Aylmer a failed scientist, as the death of his wife proves, but he is also a bad husband. His idealism is incompatible with marriage itself, as a ritual that seeks to reconcile the ideal or spiritual with the physical or sensual, as it celebrates love through the body ("The Best That Earth Could Offer," 148–49).

idealism of Brand. The "rough, heavy-looking" lime-burner, cloddish and "coal-begrimed"(85), contrasts sharply with the worn "thin ... thoughtful visage" of the returning wayfarer, whose eyes, Hawthorne writes, "gleamed like fires within the entrance of a mysterious cavern" (86). Indeed, Hawthorne speculates that Brand's long occupation as lime-burner may have fueled his obsession. It is such a solitary and "thoughtful" task, he writes, that the long watching of the intense glow of flames may have melted his thoughts "into the one idea that took possession of his life" (84).

Brand's speculative nature is further set apart from the sensuality and baser modes of thought of the ordinary run of humanity as he is contrasted with the villagers whom Bartram invites to visit the returning traveler. The stage-agent, lawyer, and village doctor are each described as formerly productive members of a community who have since been ruined due to the circumstances of accident and fleshly indulgence in food and drink. Described collectively as "red-nosed" and "purple-visaged," wild, maimed, desperate, and rude (91), they nevertheless maintain a degree of dignity and elicit sympathy from the reader, as they maintain their contact with human society. Lawyer Giles, Hawthorne notes, despite this "or any previous stage of his misfortunes ... still kept up the courage and spirit of a man ... [fighting] a stern battle against want and hostile circumstances" (92). Similarly, the village Doctor, despite the cases of misdiagnosis hinted at by Hawthorne, was still supposed by the community to possess "such wonderful skill, such native gifts of healing," that it would not let him sink beneath its reach (92). These characters, then, taken together, serve Hawthorne as representative of a dignified but diminished humanity; they are weak, fallible, and incomplete in themselves, yet they are members of a community from which Brand's excessive pride and egoism have alienated him. As Hawthorne writes, Brand wished to distinguish himself from ordinary, sinful humanity by committing the one crime "beyond the scope of Heaven's else infinite mercy" (88).

In his characterization of Brand, then, and the contrast that he draws between Brand and the villagers, Hawthorne points up the distinction between petty sins of the flesh, such as sensual indulgence, and spiritual or rarefied evil. This latter he defines, through Brand, as the triumph of the intellect over the heart, as, in an effort to assume god-like knowledge and power in the commission of monstrous sin, Brand himself becomes monstrous, alienated from the human community. As a result, he lacks the ability to show compassion for his fellow humans, as he lacks the recognition of his own common humanity. "Leave me," he says bitterly to the three villagers, "ye brute beasts, that have made yourselves so, shrivelling up your souls with fiery liquors! I have done with you. Years and years ago, I groped into your hearts and found nothing there for my purpose. Get ye gone!" (93). As Brand sits in judgment over the hearts of his fellows, he supplants God's will with his own and fails to recognize what Hawthorne defines as the sacredness of the human heart. The Unpardonable Sin, defined by the Gospel of Matthew as "blasphemy against the Holy Ghost," becomes, for Hawthorne, as he records in his notebook in 1844, "a want of love and reverence for the Human Soul."[22] As the soul or human heart can be understood as the dwelling place of the sacred, the source of our knowledge of God, the unpardonable sin can be viewed as the banishing of God from creation. Thus, undermining any inherent sacredness as basis for his own reverence for creation, Brand ceases to "partake of the universal

---

[22] Nathaniel Hawthorne, *American Notebooks*, 251. In his study of the American romance tradition, Chase observes that Hawthorne's judgment against those who violate the human heart is as harsh as that of Cooper and Faulkner against those men who "plunder and exploit the land that Providence put into the trust of Americans." He writes that for Hawthorne, "as for them, violation, or impiety, is the worst of crimes" (*The American Novel,* 78).

throb" of human sympathy and compassion (99). As God or demon, he rises above or falls below "the magnetic chain of humanity," as he investigates the hearts and souls of humankind for the "Unpardonable Sin." The consequence of this act of abstraction, of course, is that he commits the "Sin" himself, as he reduces people to mere objects of his study, manipulating them as "puppets" for his research (99).

Ethan Brand, then, commits, as do Hawthorne's other idealists, the act of abstraction and consequent objectification that lies within the peculiar precinct of the scientist, artist, and aesthete. In the name of reform, perfection, and power, the scientist/idealists attempt to transcend history, flesh, and fleshly limitation, in order to come to know, and hence assume control over, the object of their investigation. As they aspire to surpass the boundaries of nature, they abandon their ties to humanity. The knowledge of nature assumed by the scientist or artist, then, which allows them to duplicate or represent its processes, breeds power which, lacking a correspondent development of the heart, places them in constant danger of destroying their subjects. As Hawthorne has shown, such a transcendent perspective is not only dangerous; it is naïve. As his formulation of the romance tradition asserts, we live in a "twilight region"[23] of knowledge, a "neutral territory" in which subject is not easily separated from object, knower from known. In "Ethan Brand," the example of Esther, whom Brand has "wasted" and "absorbed" in the process of his research (94), serves as a reminder of the possible human cost of the scientistic mode of knowing. The spectacle of the old dog

---

[23] ———, *The French and Italian Notebooks* in vol. 14, *The Centenary Edition of the Works of Nathaniel Hawthorne* (Columbus: Ohio State University Press, 1980) 285.

chasing its unnaturally short tail further speaks to the futility of assuming method as a sound model for understanding the human heart, as its dualism effectively places mind in an unending war with matter.

# 2

## PURITANS AND MODERN METHODISM

Hawthorne's relationship to and feelings toward the Puritans have been well documented. It is a well-known fact of Hawthorne scholarship, for instance, that he changed his name from Hathorne to Hawthorne in order to dissociate himself from his great grandfather, Judge Hathorne, who was a presiding judge in the Salem witchcraft trials as well as a persecutor of the Quakers. Much of Hawthorne's fiction evokes Puritan settings and reveals a close acquaintanceship with Puritan theology and doctrine. His admiration for the moral earnestness and independent spirit of his own and his region's ancestors is apparent in such sketches as "The Gray Champion" and "Endicott and the Red Cross." Further, his quarrel with the idealism of the New England Transcendentalists, as indicated in the previous chapter, would suggest a closer affinity with the Puritans—their religious forebears—whose Calvinist doctrine had been diluted and ultimately rejected under the influence of eighteenth-century rationalism and nineteenth-century Romanticism.[1] Indeed, as Hyatt Waggoner has argued in his study of the religious and philosophical assumptions that underlie Hawthorne's aesthetics, Hawthorne believed the Puritan doctrine of natural depravity, despite its severity, to be a more accurate understanding of human nature than that suggested by the

---

[1] Although my understanding of Puritan theology and the American religious and intellectual currents that shaped Hawthorne's fiction have been gleaned from a variety of sources, the most helpful have been Hyatt H. Waggoner's *Hawthorne: A Critical Study* and Henry Pochmann's survey, *Masters of American Literature*.

optimism and ideals of the Transcendentalists.[2] What Hawthorne rejected in the Puritans was the religious intolerance, and consequent lack of charity, that characterized their attempt to purge their society of human evil, in order to establish a reformed church in their New World colony. While Hawthorne's rejection of Puritan intolerance is evident in enough tales and sketches to be universally acknowledged among scholars, what this study seeks to demonstrate is the relevance of Hawthorne's treatment of the Puritans to an ongoing critique of modern scientism. This chapter will therefore re-describe Hawthorne's traditional dichotomies—between head and heart, law and nature—as instances of the subjectivism of modern method.

An understanding of the Puritans' cosmology can assist in understanding the intolerance that characterizes their worldview. In his study of *The Scarlet Letter* Charles Feidelson Jr. describes the reformist zeal of the Puritans in terms of the alienation that characterized the new modern consciousness in the post-Medieval secular world. The advances of science that banished God from the world as a coherent center of creation, he argues, created a series of disjunctions that fractured the Puritans' understanding of self and cosmos.[3] The consequence of this modern fragmentation that separates God and nature, self and society, and mind and body is dramatized by Hawthorne as the dualisms that pervade *The Scarlet Letter* and his works set within the Puritan context, generally. His Puritans, assuming this modern dualism as their metaphysical model, attempt to rid themselves of nature, the corruption mandated by mortality and sex, for instance, in order to establish the earthly reign of a banished God through religious and civil law. Seen in this light, then, the Puritans were reformers

---

[2] Hyatt H. Waggoner, *Hawthorne: A Critical Study*, rev. ed. (Cambridge MA: Belknap-Harvard University Press, 1963) 15.

[3] Charles Feidelson Jr., "The Scarlet Letter," in *Hawthorne's Centenary Essays*, ed. Roy Harvey Pearce (Columbus: Ohio State University Press, 1964) 33.

whose earthly Utopia rested on the confidence of modern rationalism to understand human nature, to name and therefore contain, the world outside the mind. The Puritans manifest the same spiritual and intellectual pride that characterizes Hawthorne's other idealists. Similar to his scientists and artists, they exhibit an autonomous subjectivity that seeks to know, and therefore to ultimately control, history.

From the opening pages of *The Scarlet Letter*, the dualism of the Puritan world is apparent. [4] The "grim rigidity" that hardens the faces of the magistrates and townspeople as they look toward the "iron-clamped oaken door" of the prison that holds Hester Prynne suggests the resolve with which they enforce the laws of their New World colony of "human virtue and happiness" (47–49). The wild rosebush that blooms next to the prison door, however, as well as Hawthorne's careful notation of the shadowy wilderness that borders the small settlement, points to the reality of nature and, therefore, to the inability of the Puritans to accomplish the task of erasing or bending the world of matter to the dictates of their will. The images of dualism thus introduced in the first few pages of the novel underscore its root conflict: the inevitable reality of both mind and matter, and the necessary co-existence, therefore, of both law and nature. Similarly, the existence of the prison and the cemetery, both built early on in the establishment of the colony, points to Hawthorne's narrative irony regarding the Puritan project of starting over, of cleansing human nature of its complexity, its sexuality, and the limitations imposed by mortality.

Here, then, as in his other works, Hawthorne conceives human nature to be a mixture of both good and evil. To assume otherwise, to attempt to apprehend the complexity of human nature rationally, is to assume a standpoint outside of human history that objectifies the physical world. His Puritan magistrates,

---

[4] Nathaniel Hawthorne, *The Scarlet Letter* in vol. 1, *The Centenary Edition of the Works of Nathaniel Hawthorne* (Columbus: Ohio State University Press, 1965).

like his other scientifically minded theoreticians, rule by abstractions. They drag Hester's iniquity "into the sunshine"; branding her with the scarlet letter, they set her apart as a type, a universal sign of human frailty, and designate her as a "living sermon against sin" (63). Attempting to isolate her human nature, the magistrates thus deny their own "common nature" (55). Similar to Hawthorne's other reformers, they lose an essential aspect of their own humanity as they sacrifice their ability to show compassion to a fellow creature in order to meet the demands of their ideal. Employing sexual imagery that adequately conveys the objectifying consequences of the methodological means by which they seek to control her nature, Hawthorne writes that, standing Hester on the scaffold, the Puritan magistrates attempt to "force her to lay open her heart's secrets in … broad daylight " (65). As this rape imagery suggests, they violate the "mystery of [this] woman's soul" (66–67), as they bring the tenets of their abstract and legalistic code to bear on the "mesh of good and evil" (64) that constitutes her human nature.[5] As Hawthorne shows, in their treatment of Hester Prynne the magistrates therefore reduce the difficult existential "question of human guilt, passion, and anguish" (65) to fit the categories of their cool rational analysis.

The Puritan townspeople are not the only characters who suffer from the subject/object dichotomy that afflicts the modern consciousness. Each of the main characters of the novel manifests this fragmented or alienated modern sensibility. Chillingworth, for instance, is Hawthorne's stock figure of detached scientific intelligence, a physician who, intent on revenge, delves into the secrets of Dimmesdale's heart like a miner after gold (129). Confident of the autonomy of his "self-relying intelligence," he "scrutinizes" his patient's soul, "delving among his principles," in order to

---

[5] In language similar to my own in strength, Nina Baym notes Hawthorne's sympathy with such strong female characters as Hester Prynne in their struggles against a "murderous male authority" ("Revisiting Hawthorne's Feminism" in *Hawthorne and the Real,* 108).

discover and then intensify Dimmesdale's secret guilt (124). Hawthorne writes that Chillingworth thus becomes not merely a spectator, but a player in the drama of human guilt and remorse that is played out before him, manipulating Dimmesdale's emotions in order to satisfy his own ends.

Chillingworth's role as player or manipulator is enabled by the aesthetic consciousness that, as we have seen, characterizes Hawthorne's artist figures and scientists, generally. Describing himself as homeless, "a wanderer" (76), before he arrives in the New England colony in search of Hester, he possesses the capacity, demonstrated by Coverdale, to occupy another's mind, without empathy, and, thus, to come to know objectively the human "life-tide" that passes transparently before him (125). Unaffected by emotion regarding Dimmesdale's suffering, he comes to possess him; as he had prophesied to Hester—"he shall be mine!" (76). As Chillingworth lacks human sympathy and a place in the human community, Hawthorne writes that he becomes "unhumanized," as he penetrates the secrets of another's soul. He consequently withers up and "shrivelle[s] away" like an "uprooted weed" at the novel's end, having become nothing more than a sign of the evil principle he embodies. (260).

The character of Dimmesdale provides Chillingworth with an easy victim. A young Puritan priest in the New World colony, he proves himself unable to live out existentially the doctrines regarding the understanding of human nature formulated by his church. Educated and enlightened, and, therefore, serving Hawthorne as representative of the reformed church in the modern world, he embodies the mind/body dualism that the church perpetuates as it seeks to establish the reign of its heavenly kingdom on earth. Feidelson has demonstrated that in a world that no longer knows an immanent God, the Puritans seek reconciliation with a lost God by focusing on this disjunction, or condition of disinheritance.[6] He argues that, in an attempt to aspire to pure spirit, their Manichean theology subjugates the world of matter to that of spirit, and the desires and demands of the flesh in the individual to the rule of law, mind, or reason (33). Thus, Dimmesdale manifests this modern disjunction, formalized by the creeds of his church, in the torment that overcomes him when his passional nature drives him to commit adultery with Hester Prynne, and the self-abnegation caused by his religious belief, as well as his own lack of moral fortitude, prevents him from the public confession that would relieve his agony.

The Manichean root of Dimmesdale's modern sensibility is apparent from his first introduction in terms that suggest a basic alienation from the human community and the dichotomy between his physical and spiritual natures. He is described as a young, promising religious scholar of "very striking aspect, with a white, lofty, and impending brow" who, despite "his high native gifts and scholarlike attainments," nevertheless has about him "an apprehensive ... startled ... look"; he appears lost on the "pathway of human existence" (66). While the devoted members of his congregation mistake his tremulous manner, his pale, emaciated cheeks, and his large, melancholy eyes as evidence of a tender and pure spirit and of ascetic practice meant to purge his earthly nature, he, in fact, suffers the pangs of an introspective Puritan conscience obsessed with secret sin. His guilty conscience is

---

[6] Feidelson, "The Scarlet Letter," 34. Baym makes a similar point. She observes that God is virtually absent from the text. "Divinity in this romance is a remote, vague, ceremonially invoked concept that functions chiefly to sanction and support the secular power of the Puritan rulers." What we have, she argues, in the absence of God, is "a self-satisfied secular autocracy." This is important thematically for the romance, as what Hester and Dimmesdale commit is not a crime against "divine law," but rather it is a "social crime" (*Shape of Hawthorne's Career*, 125). This distinction, Baym argues, allows Hawthorne to investigate the set of contrasts between private and public, individual and society, female and male, or the repression of the female by a patriarchal Puritan regime.

exacerbated by his inability to confess his sin and, therefore, gain the reconciliation earned by a penitent. Hawthorne writes that as "Remorse" drives him to confess, "Cowardice" invariably draws him back, and the two competing impulses twist his life into an "inextricable knot ... of heaven-defying guilt and vain repentance" (148). Described as an earnest and principled man who "adore[s] the truth" (143), Dimmesdale is unable to rest in the hypocrisy that his lack of courage drives him to. Further, as he embodies the moral absolutism of the Puritan dichotomy of good and evil and is unable to accept the existence of sin within himself, he believes himself unfit to minister to the needs of the people. "What can a ruined soul like mine effect towards the redemption of other souls?" he asks Hester, "or a polluted soul, towards their purification?" (191). Loving the truth, then, and dwelling on the contrast between "what [he] seem[s] and what [he is]," he becomes, in his own eyes, insubstantial and inauthentic. He is consequently filled with self-loathing and self-pity and becomes increasingly estranged from the community. Ironically, as Hawthorne notes of his preaching ability, this same sharing in the sinful inheritance of humanity gives his sermons their sympathy and power to mingle with "the great heart of mankind" (243).

The tale thus ends tragically for Dimmesdale, as he fully embodies the dehumanizing consequences of the Puritan dichotomy of good and evil as it attempts to address the complexity of divided human nature. In the concluding chapter of the novel, he enters the holiday processional intent on delivering his election sermon, and, seemingly, shut off from the sights and sounds of the life of the community around him. He appears completely "abstracted" (239), closed off even to Hester herself with whom he has just verbally renewed his covenant in the forest. (His "unsympathizing thoughts," she fears, remove him completely "from their mutual world" [239–40].) His sermon is the typical Puritan jeremiad, a ringing endorsement of the ideals of

the Puritans as it foretells their future success in the New World.[7]
He ends the sermon, however—as Hawthorne notes of this man
who has just attained "the very proudest eminence of superiority"
allotted only to New England's clergy (249)—with his head bent
forward upon the cushion of the pulpit. Emotionally and
physically exhausted, and with Hester Prynne placed strategically
by Hawthorne on the platform of the scaffold below him, he
appears unable to bear the burdens of office, much less those of
history. His final death further manifests this utter irreconcilability
between the law that rules him and his own human nature. As he
discloses the scarlet letter upon his breast and confesses his guilt
to the multitude, he is, he believes, reconciled to a merciful God
who grants pardon to even the "vilest of sinners" (246). Given the
metaphysical structure he assumes and the moral choices it
mandates, he is thus granted a victory, in death if not in life,
according to the uncompromising doctrine of his Puritan belief.[8]

In his characterization of Hester Prynne, Hawthorne develops
the impulsive, passional nature of Dimmesdale that Puritan
doctrine suppresses. Cast out from society as a public emblem of
sin, she nevertheless possesses all of the "natural dignity and force
of character" that Dimmesdale lacks (52). In the opening scene of

---

[7] In *The American Jeremiad*, Sacvan Bercovitch argues that the Puritan
fathers adapted the traditional European formula of the jeremiad as rhetorical
device to incorporate the ideas of their New World enterprise. The Puritan
clergy moved beyond the jeremiad as traditional lament over earthly trials
and tribulations in order to urge their listeners to interpret earthly trial as an
indication of their chosen-ness as God's people. Bercovitch concludes that
the American jeremiad is to be distinguished from its European model on the
basis of its intrinsic optimism, intended to instill within its hearers faith in the
ideals of the Puritan enterprise of establishing a reformed Church in the New
World. In this way, the American jeremiad was not only a central rhetorical
strategy used by the Puritans to advance their "errand in the wilderness," but
served as well to ground the "myth of America," generally (Preface xi).

[8] Edward Wagenknecht makes this same point. Although Dimmesdale's
victory is a limited one, given the constraints of his religious belief, it is,
nevertheless, a victory.

the drama, Prynne issues forth from the prison door under the guard of the town beadle, but repels him on the threshold, in order to face the stern stares of the townspeople of "her own free will." She is described physically by Hawthorne as tall with "dark and abundant hair" and "a marked brow and deep black eyes" that, contrasted with Hawthorne's blond "innocents," suggest a natural regal bearing, strength of will and character. Similarly, the scarlet letter itself, in Hester's hands, has been embellished by art, embroidered round with "fantastic flourishes of gold thread," manifesting her own "fertility and gorgeous luxuriance of fancy" (52). Hester thus appears to the Puritan townspeople as the very type of passional nature, imagination, and individual freedom that would defy their law. Branding her with the scarlet letter for her act of adultery, they banish her to a small cottage "on the outskirts of town" where she is no longer a threat to their civilization (81).

Characterized by Hawthorne according to her sexual—and hence from the Puritan perspective, sinful—nature, Hester Prynne embodies the anarchic, antinomian impulses that threaten civic law in this Puritan community. He compares her to the historical Ann Hutchinson, a feminist and religious freethinker, who was exiled for heresy in the early years of the Puritan colony. He describes the rosebush that blooms next to the prison door as rumored to have "sprung up under the footsteps of the sainted Ann Hutchinson" (48). Later in the text, he notes that if it were not for the care of little Pearl, which keeps Hester somewhat within the confines of conventional domestic life, she "might have come down to us in history, hand in hand with Ann Hutchinson, as the foundress of a religious sect," or a "prophetess" (165). In this pairing with Hutchinson, then, Hawthorne ironically attributes characteristics to Hester that will align her with the idealism represented by his Puritans. The imagination and native sagacity with which he credits her serves ultimately to increase her isolation from the community that the wearing of the scarlet letter had originally imposed. Her "long seclusion from society," he writes, had "little accustomed [her] to measure her ideas of right and wrong by any standard external to herself." "Standing alone in the world," as he describes her, "she [had] cast away the fragments of a broken chain. The world's law was no law for her mind" (164). Her isolation, then, engenders a "freedom of speculation" that Hawthorne ultimately identifies with a belief in an emergent doctrine of progress:

> It was an age in which the human intellect, newly emancipated, had taken a more active and a wider range than for many centuries before. Men of the sword had overthrown nobles and kings. Men bolder than these had overthrown and rearranged—not actually, but within the sphere of theory ... the whole system of ancient prejudice, wherewith was linked much of ancient principle. Hester Prynne imbibed this spirit. (164)

Thus cut off from the community by the wearing of the scarlet letter, Hawthorne writes that Hester's heart loses "its regular and healthy throb" (166). Her life turns from one of passion and feeling to one of thought, and she comes to embody in herself the imbalance of thought and feeling, head and heart, characteristic of Hawthorne's nineteenth-century idealists and other modern theoreticians.[9] Exemplifying this Emersonian

---

[9] This change in Hester invites a range of critical speculation. Richard Chase attributes the loss of emotion here to Hester's growing feminism. "Once a luxurious and passionate woman," he writes, "Hester takes up a life of renunciation and service.... [I]n her lonely life, Hester becomes a radical." He continues: "She even comes to think in feminist rhetoric, and one can hear not only Hester but Miss Peabody [Hawthorne's sister-in-law Elizabeth] and Margaret Fuller talking firmly about 'the whole relation between man and woman'" (*The American Novel*, 73). (From a post-sixties reference point regarding matters of gender, one would have to wonder here about Chase's use of the term "firmly" to characterize the hypothetical conversation between these two feminist women.) Baym offers a much more nuanced account of Hawthorne's treatment of Hester's feminism as she notes the loss of imagination, passion, and impulse—traits associated with women—under

doctrine of self-reliance, she exhorts Dimmesdale during their meeting in the forest to "begin all anew"—to give up his name even and "make [himself] another"—and to join her in escaping from the Puritan colony, into the forest or across the sea (197–98). She thus reveals her confidence that, by escaping the repressive constraints of Puritan law and human institution, they can escape the reality of their human nature, and the entanglements it will cause. Though Hawthorne is obviously sympathetic to Hester's predicament, condemning in his vivid portrayal of the Puritans' moral absolutism, their self-righteousness more than her and Dimmesdale's adultery, Hester's lonely life and death do not suggest such an easy reconciliation between law and nature, or the ability, believed in by Hester, as well as by the Puritans, to bend or escape human nature and history by an effort of the will.

As he dramatizes the Transcendentalist assumptions behind Hester's thought, then, Hawthorne shows both her own and the Puritans' responses to the conflict between law and nature to be inherently modern and methodological as they seek to privilege mind over matter, subject over object, in an effort to control human behavior and destiny. The other characters also demonstrate the poles of the subject/object dualism of historical modernity as they are manifest in the law and nature dichotomy that rules the Puritan world.[10] While the Puritans seek to name and

---

the legalistic and patriarchal rule of the Puritans. She further points out that since women were of "less account" in this society than men, Hester suffers a physical punishment, rather than the psychological torment experienced by Dimmesdale. She is branded with the scarlet letter, banished, and "left alone ... to develop as she will" (*Shape of Hawthorne's Career*, 129). This is, then, how she develops. For a reading similar to my own that sees in Hester's evolution a critique of Transcendentalist idealism, see Waggoner.

[10] In his characterization of Pearl, Hawthorne intensifies the lawlessness and natural impulse of Hester. Described as sprite-like, an elf- or fairy-child, she appears intangible, remote, and capricious. As Hester lavishly attires her child, she becomes the living embodiment of the scarlet letter. As Dimmesdale states, she knows no governing principle, but "the freedom of a broken law" (134). Wholly natural and therefore not human, then, Hawthorne

thereby contain human nature, branding Hester with the scarlet letter and banishing her to the fringes of their civilized society, Hester insists on the primacy of the individual's right to live outside the confines imposed by the laws of society. Hawthorne's judgment on the Puritans' lack of charity, as well as the lonely life that Hester's action causes her to endure, suggests that neither response does justice to the complexity of human nature. If the Puritans see only evil in the world, Hester focuses only on the good. Embodying what will become Emerson's doctrine of American self-reliance and the optimism of the Transcendentalist movement, in general, she expresses her belief in the potential divinity of the individual ("What we did has a consecration of its own!" [195]) and in the ability to reconstruct self and society anew. Ultimately denying the entanglements of human history, then, Hester's confidence in progress is as dualistic as the Puritan impulse to constrain human nature as the source of evil. If the Puritans fixate upon evil, Hester would deny the reality of sin, or the limitations imposed by nature. Against such idealism, the ending of Hawthorne's romance—Dimmesdale's inevitable death and Hester's lonely life—suggests that Hawthorne himself believed law and nature, self and society, and the human head and heart, to be in unending and inevitable, and, therefore, tragic conflict.[11] Here, then, is the explicit "moral": "Be true! Be true!

---

writes that Pearl needs a grief to "humanize" her (184). At Dimmesdale's death, as his confession has moved her to acknowledge him as her father, she seems to suffer this grief, and thus undergoes the transition from abstract principle to historical human being, capable of thought and feeling. Consequently, at novel's end, Hawthorne suggests of this weak and two-imensional character that she will grow to be a "woman" in the world, possibly proving herself capable of "human joy and sorrow" (256).

[11] Critics, by and large, and regardless of critical school or disposition, agree on this issue of the irreconcilability of these poles, and, therefore, that the romance ends in tragedy. See, for instance, Baym and Waggoner. While Baym locates the conflict within its Romantic context as that which arises between repressive society and aspects of the private self (*Shape of Hawthorne's Career*), Waggoner moves beyond this critique of the

Be true! Show freely to the world, if not your worst, yet some trait whereby the worst may be inferred!" (260). Such an admonition would suggest that we cultivate qualities of character that are true to our common nature and that enable the life of community.

If the principle characterizations of *The Scarlet Letter* reveal the dualism that underlies not only Puritan theology but also its nineteenth-century incarnation in American Transcendentalism, in "Young Goodman Brown," Hawthorne further demonstrates the false bottom to such idealism as it is shown to quickly devolve into a cynicism equally destructive to human community.[12] In this frequently anthologized story, rich symbolism combines with Hawthorne's use of the journey motif to render, in poignant and concise terms, the story of the undoing of his young idealist. The story begins as Goodman Brown, a young Puritan Everyman, leaves his home and his wife "Faith" in Salem village to venture at dusk into the forest on what he describes as an errand of "evil purpose" (75). Once in the woods, he meets his guide for the journey, a stranger whom, as he carries a walking stick that "wriggles" and as he manifests other clues that suggest his supernaturalism, Brown and the reader soon discover to be the Devil. As they walk along, Brown grows wary of the shadows and the deepening dusk of the forest and explains to the Devil that he is beginning to have "scruples" regarding his engagement with evil, and regrets that he has left his "Faith," even temporarily, on such an errand (76). He is reassured by the Devil that he is not the first of his Puritan race of "honest men and good Christians" who

---

irresolvable difference between the adulterers and Puritan law in his broad understanding of the religious and philosophical notions that inform Hawthorne's work. Regardless of time and place, Hester and Dimmesdale would suffer conflicts due to the claims of both their moral and natural selves. A happier political climate, or a reformed, more egalitarian society, as Hester wishes for, would not solve this age-old dilemma of the divided self.

[12] Nathaniel Hawthorne, "Young Goodman Brown," in *Mosses from an Old Manse* in vol. 10, *The Centenary Edition of the Works of Nathaniel Hawthorne* (Columbus: Ohio State University Press, 1974).

have kept a rendezvous with him. In confirmation of this fact, Brown soon discovers other members of the community, notably his catechist Goody Cloyse, the minister, and the pious Deacon Gookin, in the forest with him and wonders at their own presence in the wilderness "where no church had ever been gathered, nor solitary Christian prayed" (82). Dismayed by the presence of his townspeople, and inferring the blackness of the human heart, generally, from this fact, he lifts his hands to pray—"With Heaven above, and Faith below," he cries, "I will yet stand firm against the devil"—as "a black mass of cloud" sweeps overhead and obstructs his view of the heavens (82). From the cloud he hears a "confused and doubtful sound of voices," those of villagers he had met at the "communion-table" mingling with those who "riot[ed] at the tavern," and he hears the sad and lamenting voice of a young woman as well (82). Recognizing his wife's voice among this black cloud of voices, of the pious and impious alike, he calls her name in despair as a pink hair ribbon flutters down from the sky in answer to him. "'My Faith is gone!' [he cries], after one stupefied moment. 'There is no good on earth and sin is but a name. Come, devil! for to thee is this world given'" (83). Mad with despair, then, he rushes on through the night and through the wilderness, abandoned to his own evil purpose and to the evil that he perceives to pervade the world. He comes at last to a witch-meeting, set in a clearing of the woods, at which are gathered all the village townspeople, ready to welcome him and his wife Faith to the "communion of [their] race," into an awareness, that is, of the ubiquity of sin as the "nature and destiny of humankind" (86). "By the sympathy of your human hearts for sin," the celebrant tells them, "ye shall scent out all the places … where crime has been committed" (87). Indeed, they will become, as he further tells them, more conscious of the "secret guilt of others, both in deed and thought," than they are of their own (88). Consequently, as a result of his experience, Goodman Brown returns to the village the following morning, "a stern … sad, [and] darkly meditative …

man" (89). A confirmed Puritan, convinced of the depravity of the human heart, he is henceforth unable to participate in the community life—to attend church, to converse on the streets—for his suspicion of evil in every heart, including that of his beloved "Faith."

The significance of the story, of course, lies in the fact that Hawthorne suggests that Brown has dreamed his whole experience in the woods. "Had Goodman Brown fallen asleep in the forest, and only dreamed a wild dream of a witch-meeting?" he asks near the end of his tale (89). Indeed, throughout the story, Brown's objective perceptions are continuously couched in fantasy and called into question. The story is set (as are so many of Hawthorne's stories) in the unclear atmosphere of twilight and dusk and in a shadowy wilderness of vague sights and sounds. Brown hears the voices of the minister and Deacon Gookin in the forest, but cannot see them through the gloom. The black cloud of voices "hurrie[s] across the zenith" of an otherwise blue sky and on a windless night (82), and even the pink ribbon that Brown identifies with Faith is merely "something" that "fluttered lightly down through the air, and caught on the branch of a tree" (83). On the other hand, Brown's own evil intentions are made clear from the beginning. As stated earlier, he acknowledges the evil intention of his adventure in the wilderness. Regarding the trust that his wife Faith shows in him as he embarks on his errand, he remarks, "What a wretch am I to leave her on such an errand! ... Well; she's a blessed angel on earth; and after this one night, I'll cling to her skirts and follow her to Heaven" (75). There is ample evidence in the story, then, to suggest that the events of the evening did not literally happen, and that Brown, having discovered the propensity for evil within himself, projects it onto others and onto the world around him. The narrative irony thus points to the problem inherent in Brown's own idealization of religious faith, represented in the story by his wife "Faith." Since he cannot accept the possibility of evil within himself or his wife, he cannot live with the reality of evil in the world, as his subsequent behavior attests. Hawthorne suggests that in a worldview so dominated by the idea of evil, escaped only through absolute faith, in a worldview, that is, so dichotomized, there can be no hope or redemption. The story of "Young Goodman Brown" is, then, like *The Scarlet Letter*, "not a story about a sin but about the consequences of a sin."[13] It is about the existential reality of human sinfulness within the context of a worldview unable to come to terms with it. Accordingly, as a story of initiation, "Young Goodman Brown" assumes the form of a journey from innocence to experience where the ideal is tested by the real, or the actual, and the mind is made to answer to matter. The moral point of Hawthorne's story of Brown's initiation is further enhanced by his own formulation of the romance genre as asserting a "neutral territory" against the confidence of rationalism and the claims of literary realism. The romance, he explains, conveys a twilight region in which the ideal and the real cannot be separated, and, therefore, reality cannot be apprehended positively. Just as Brown's perceptions cannot be objectively verified, the truth of the human heart, as Hester's plight demonstrates, must always remain a mystery. Hawthorne's mimetic technique, therefore, underscores his critique of the Puritans' moral absolutism. As their religious idealism is shown ultimately to result in a subjectivism that diminishes the world around them, Hawthorne calls into

---

[13] Edward Wagenknecht, *Nathaniel Hawthorne: The Man, His Tales and Romances* (New York: Continuum, 1989) 63. Hyatt Waggoner also addresses this issue of the consequences of sin or sinfulness in Hawthorne's fiction. He notes that as many of Hawthorne's stories originate from some vague or obscure source of guilt, or with a guilty act that is not dramatized— Hester's adultery, for instance, occurs before the opening of the novel— Hawthorne shifts the focus to the guilt, or "original sin," inherent in humanity, generally. Sinfulness is thus seen in Hawthorne's fiction as an existential condition, or common lot, the recognition of which ought to engender certain values, such as charity and compassion.

question the efficacy of their modern methodological understanding of human nature.

3

## ROMANCE AS BILDUNG:
## SELF-TRANSFORMATION IN *THE MARBLE FAUN*

In his seminal study, *The American Novel and Its Tradition*, Richard Chase defines the American romance in terms pertinent to Hawthorne's formulation of the genre.[1] Adopting Hawthorne's own definition of romance as a "neutral territory," Chase argues that the romance genre reflects contradictions that are unique to American culture. Distinguishing the American "romance-novel" from the English domestic novel, which is traditionally defined as concerned with issues of social life, manners, and class, Chase explains that the American novel has historically represented the situation of the individual outside the bounds of society. The dualism of American Puritan theology, for instance, which places the individual in direct relation with God, as well as the frontier conditions of the New World, have left Americans as individuals free from convention, and, therefore, in a relation to God, nature, and society unmediated by tradition. Such a condition of solitariness, even alienation, Chase argues, has led the American imagination to re-examine questions of ultimate concern, to grapple with the eternal struggle between good and evil, for instance, and with aspects of human experience and human nature untouched by the civilizing force of the domestic novel.[2] As it

---

[1] Richard Chase, *The American Novel and Its Tradition* (New York: Gordian, 1957).

[2] Among American theorists, Leo Marx has formulated the difference between the American romance-novel and the English domestic novel in a similar way. He argues that contradictions in values displayed by the figure

confronts these fundamental issues, the American romance has traditionally concerned itself with the inner life of individuals, with questions of human psychology and moral nature. This interest in interiority and moral life would suggest, then, that romance is the genre best suited to Hawthorne's interest in portraying "the truth of the human heart." His stories of initiation involve a process of discovery in which characters and reader are continually confronted by the "boundless sphere" of the heart and are returned to a recognition of self in which finitude is recognized as the central experience of humanity. It is this recognition of the limited nature of humanity, the divided nature of the self, and the reality of sin and suffering, that Hawthorne's romances share with the Christian myth of the Fall.[3]

Of all Hawthorne's works, *The Marble Faun* is most overtly and self-consciously a story of the Fall.[4] The story, of course, centers on four friends, one of whom, because he resembles the bust of the Faun of Praxiteles, is believed, half-seriously by the others, to have furry ears and to be descended from that race of fauns or woodland creatures who dwelt in Arcadia. Donatello is, therefore, supposed by his friends to be half human and half beast and occupies a position of mythic importance, both for them and for the novel, as he signifies that prelapsarian innocence where the human and the natural meet and co-mingle harmoniously. The story develops as Donatello commits murder, out of love for Miriam, losing his innocence, but at the same time acquiring

---

of the solitary American are attributable, in nineteenth-century American fiction, to the rapid changes to life brought about by technology, by the sudden and revolutionary incursion of the "machine" into the American garden. The rapid changes caused by technology spurred on questions of morality, as indeed they do today.

[3] The relationship of Hawthorne's themes to the story of the "Fall" has been a long-standing observation of Hawthorne scholarship.

[4] Nathaniel Hawthorne, *The Marble Faun,* in vol. 4, *The Centenary Edition of the Works of Nathaniel Hawthorne* (Columbus: Ohio State University Press, 1968).

humanity as he is transformed through his encounter with sin and his experience of suffering into a man of thought and feeling. His characterization thus serves Hawthorne as a means by which we may contemplate our essential dividedness, but it also points the way toward the possibility of some sort of reconciliation, or redemption.

As in *The Scarlet Letter*, the thematic significance of the story lies in Hawthorne's portrayal of his major characters, in this case, in their responses to Donatello's crime.[5] Miriam, an accomplice in the crime, is Hawthorne's tragic figure—another Hester Prynne or Zenobia. It is at the bidding of her eyes—or at least moved by an expression that he thinks he finds there—that Donatello flings her tormentor over the precipice to his death. Miriam is an exotic beauty (of Jewish, Italian, and English descent), an outsider of mysterious origin, described as prideful, passionate, melancholy, and self-reliant (95). A painter, Miriam fills her studio with sketches and paintings of direful and passionate scenes from scripture of unrequited and thwarted love, and of happy domestic scenes in which a solitary woman is always figured apart, looking on. Hawthorne tells us that she carries the weight of some unknown emotional burden from her past—knowledge of a crime, perhaps, in which she is implicated and through which she is inextricably tied to her persecutor, an artist's model who shows up in the catacombs of Rome and pursues her throughout the novel. His presence reminds her, in terms characteristic of Hawthorne, that through their common crime their "fates cross and are entangled" (95). She is thus, by virtue of the experience of her past with the stranger, removed from the sphere of common human interaction and innocence and becomes, for Hawthorne, the bearer of the burden of "original sin" as he

---

[5] As Richard Brodhead notes in his Introduction to the Penguin edition, the responses of the three other characters to Donatello's "founding crime" allow their "scheme of values" to be tested in "this story of the history of guilt" (xviiii).

describes it, the voice of lonely and tragic human experience. After Donatello's crime and subsequent alienation, for which Miriam feels responsible, she dedicates herself to a life of renunciation and penitence in the hopes of winning back his love or, at the least, of leading him toward spiritual growth and healing. Therefore, though Hawthorne attributes to her no conventional faith, by means of her life devoted to charitable action and her belief in the possibility of at least Donatello's, if not her own, redemption, she offers a somewhat Christian response to Donatello's "fall."[6]

Kenyon serves Hawthorne as a representative artist figure. A sculptor, he is criticized throughout the novel by both Miriam and Hilda for the aloof, cool, rational analysis he offers in response to the conflict suffered in the lives of his friends. Although a man of thought, Kenyon is referred to by Hawthorne as "a man of marble" (103). Hilda points out in chapter four, that, as a sculptor, Kenyon is more concerned with outline than expression or emotion (18), and after he is unable to hear Miriam's emotional confession of her and Donatello's guilt, she asserts that he is as "cold and pitiless as [his] ... marble." He can do nothing for her but "petrify [her] into a marble companion for [his newly wrought statue of] Cleopatra ..." (129). Therefore, though described as sensitive and sincere, possessing the "ideal forehead [and] deeply set eyes" of Hawthorne's thinker, Kenyon nevertheless privileges head over heart in Hawthorne's dichotomy and exhibits the detached intellect characteristic of the artist/intellectual, as well as the liberal spirit of Hawthorne's reformers. This is made clear in a scene in which

---

[6] Although within the scheme of values tested in the novel, Miriam's response to Donatello's "fall" can be seen as Christian, few Christian readers would recognize this representation of a diluted, and, therefore, inefficacious, faith. As Emily Budick reminds us, however, in Hawthorne's fiction, "doubt is the condition of our lives in this world"; faith therefore always includes a healthy skepticism ("Instituting the American Romance Tradition," in *Nathaniel Hawthorne's* The Scarlet Letter, 84).

he and Donatello come upon the squalid remains of an old town on their ramble through the countryside on their way to Perugia. Kenyon, echoing Holgrave in *The House of the Seven Gables*, voices his confidence in the potential for reform:

> All towns should be made capable of purification by fire, or of decay within each half-century .... We may build almost immortal habitations, it is true; but we cannot keep them from growing old, musty, unwholesome, dreary, full of death-scents, ghosts and murder-stains; in short, habitations such as one sees everywhere in Italy, be they hovels or palaces. (301–02)

"You should go with me to my native country," Kenyon continues to Donatello. "In that fortunate land, each generation has only its own sins and sorrows to bear" (302). Like Holgrave, then, he believes in the fresh start, in the ability to reconstruct human nature anew. As artist, he employs the keen insight of his imaginative art in order to assist Donatello in his emotional and spiritual struggle. He manages to capture, as he models Donatello's bust, both the hidden guilt and emotional anguish in Donatello's heart, and consequently acts as a diagnostician, advising Donatello to escape his "slothful anguish," through effort, and to turn his youthful experience of "unutterable evil" toward the end of higher spiritual and social good. It is therefore Kenyon who first voices the premises underlying the notion of the "fortunate fall" which figures so largely as a motif later in the story. As he explains to Miriam, Donatello's "bitter agony" has inspired "soul and intellect" (282) within him and "after his recent profound experience, he will recreate the world by the new eyes with which he will regard it" (284). The looming question of the "fortunate fall" is never explicitly answered by Hawthorne in the novel; however, as it is voiced by Kenyon, it is a response that allows him, as modern secular humanist, to bring rational meaning to the experience of suffering. [7]

At the other end of the moral and philosophical spectrum from both Miriam's tragic sensibility and Kenyon's rational humanism is Hilda's Puritanism. Described by Hawthorne as a "New England girl" of "white shining purity" (7), a "young American," embodying her country's innocence and idealism (54), she dwells aloft in her Virgin's tower. As this analogy would suggest, Hilda's idealism points to the remoteness or inhumanity inherent in her character.[8] Kenyon, who loves her, complains of

---

[7] This point is made by Brodhead. Kenyon's response to Donatello's "fall" and resulting spiritual and emotional anguish is that of the modern secular humanist, intent on human improvement achieved through human effort. Kenyon's scenes with Donatello in the tower, he writes, "read like the birth of modern therapeutic counseling" (xix).

[8] Of the four major characterizations, Hilda's is the most significant and problematic. Unlike Miriam and Donatello, who, at the end of the novel, are living in exile and imprisoned, respectively, Hilda is left to marry Kenyon and return to America. The fact of this happy ending for Hilda probably causes critic Conrad Shumaker to see in this "daughter of the Puritans" the "moral seriousness" necessary to America as a place of regeneration. He argues that Hawthorne attributes to woman a special role in fulfilling the destiny of America as this place of new beginning. Her "natural kindness, tenderness, and joyfulness," would temper Puritan "harshness" and ensure the Puritans' eventual success ("A Daughter of the Puritans": History in Hawthorne's *The Marble Faun*," 69). Other critics, such as Hyatt Waggoner and Terence Martin, offer more moderate praise of Hilda's character. Though they find her puritan idealism uncharitable, they nevertheless argue that Hawthorne admires her as the embodiment of the mid-nineteenth-century feminine ideal of innocence and virtue that he loved in Sophia. Similarly, Carol MacKay argues that Hilda as copyist is patterned after the "living model" of Sophia and further that her prominence in the novel allows Hawthorne to successfully explicate his central theme of copying ("Duplication and Transformation in *The Marble Faun*," *Browning, Institute Studies: An Annual of Victorian Literary and Cultural History* 12 [1984]: 110). In response to such sympathetic readings, Emily Schiller counters that an ironic distance exists between Hawthorne and his narrator that allows Hawthorne not to copy but to deconstruct this ideal of "adult, feminine

the "impression she makes of being utterly sufficient to herself ... she has no need of love!" (121), and there is a hint of criticism in Miriam's response to Hilda's suggestion that, exhilarated by the rarefied air atop her tower, she attempt a flight heavenward: "Oh, pray don't try it!" Miriam cries. "If an angel indeed, I am afraid you would never come down among us again" (54). Her Puritan idealism, as Hawthorne has portrayed it elsewhere, thus appears unhampered by any recognition of the reality of the world around her. Like Donatello, Hawthorne's other Innocent in this story, she shrinks from the gloom and darkness that surrounds the four friends in the catacombs when Miriam's "model" first reveals himself (27) and wishes to escape the "dismal" darkness back into the "blessed daylight" (25). As she emphatically thanks heaven when Miriam returns to the group of friends from the obscurity that surrounds them, her response suggests that her religious idealism does not sufficiently address the reality of Hawthorne's symbolic darkness—the real existence of death and sin in the world of which she is, by virtue of her humanity, a part.

More offensive, perhaps, to both her friends and the reader is the rigid moral absolutism that she has inherited from her Puritan past. As Miriam complains regarding her lack of sympathy for the suffering Beatrice in Guido's *Beatrice Cenci*, her "innocence is like a sharp steel sword" (66). Knowing no evil within her own heart (which Kenyon describes as "all purity and rectitude" [383]), she sees all "through the clear, crystal medium of her own integrity" (384). This uncompromising moral rectitude causes her to renounce Miriam after her commission of crime with Donatello;

---

innocence" ("The Choice of Innocence: Hilda in *The Marble Faun*," *Studies in the Novel* 26 [1994]: 379). The question of Hawthorne's attitude toward Hilda remains a very vexed one. While he certainly takes her to task for her vocation as a copyist, as it is seen to correspond with a legalism that similarly results in her judgmental attitude toward her friends, the overall treatment of his maiden, including her return home, doesn't seem to allow for any significant deconstruction of her character or values.

she begs Miriam to not come closer when her friend approaches her to confess, as she fears for her own innocence. Indeed, she fears, moments before Miriam's arrival, that her soul has indeed already been impugned by knowledge of Miriam's guilt as she perceives a likeness, never before noticed, between Beatrice's expression in the painting she has copied, and her own reflected in the mirror beside the painting. To underscore the significance of this possible discovery by Hilda of her own humanity, Miriam has already wondered, in a scene which foreshadows this one, how such a spotless soul as Hilda's could have rendered so exactly the mystery of Beatrice's suffering in her copy of Guido's famous picture.

The fact of Hilda's vocation as copyist is significant to the moral point of Hawthorne's story. Hawthorne explains that since her arrival in Rome, "Hilda had ceased to consider herself ... an original artist" (56). Instead, her great appreciation for and sympathy with the mind of the artist coupled with "a nicety and force of touch" had enabled her to produce meticulous replications of the works of the Old Masters (57). Hawthorne, therefore, writes that in any number of galleries Hilda would be seen seated before her easel in front of a work of "Guido, Domenico, Raphael," painstakingly rendering forth the "light" of the original. She is distinguished from the run of copyists, indeed, not by the measure of accuracy, but by this ability to bring forth the very "spirit and essence" of the picture (58–59), "that indefinable nothing [or] inestimable something" through which the picture acquires life and soul and therefore immortality (60). Thus, through a religious devotion to their original intention, and following precisely in their steps, Hilda manages to bring to life the ideal of the old and celebrated painters. As Hawthorne writes, "a worshipper of their genius, she wrought religiously, and therefore wrought a miracle" (60).

Hilda's desire to capture the pristine idea—the timeless essence—of the original, untainted by her own limited artistic or human perspective, would suggest that we are seeing, once again in Hawthorne's fiction, the aesthetic consciousness that Gadamer has identified in his critique of the modern scientific sensibility. Like Coverdale, who divorces himself from history, or from emotional entanglement with his friends, in order to know his subjects as objects, Hilda is also guilty of an abstraction which enables her to render forth, and hence objectify, the artistic essence that she intends to capture and convey. In introducing Hilda as a "copyist," significantly in the chapter entitled "The Virgin's Shrine"—a chapter devoted to her characterization as idealist—Hawthorne means to underscore this idealism as it bears on her artistic practice. In a romance so self-consciously devoted to a study of aesthetic theory, such attention to detail must be meaningful.[9] Indeed, in underscoring the idealism of his young copyist, Hawthorne evokes Plato's mimetic theory, which undermines the value of the work of art in the world as it claims the object of artistic effort to be the replication of a timeless, and unattainable, original. For Plato, the work of art is a mere copy of a copy thrice removed from the "form," or essence, reflected first in phenomena and second in the artistic representation.[10] Such a definition, while trivializing art by emptying it of content, likewise objectifies reality by suggesting that there is a timeless eternal to be returned to as the object of knowledge, an objective reality to be recovered or known, outside of our own historical circumstances.[11] Accordingly, as a copyist intent on replicating the

---

[9] For an article on *The Marble Faun* as aesthetic theory and dramatization of the interrelationship between art and life, see Graham Clarke.

[10] Plato, *The Republic*, trans. Paul Shorey (Cambridge MA: Harvard University Press) vol. 2, book x.

[11] Martin Kevorkian rightly identifies the violence that lies behind Platonism and the scientific discourse of the West in his analysis of the Lucretian influence on Hawthorne's fiction, though surprisingly, he doesn't extend his analysis to the obvious Platonist in Hawthorne's last novel. As she attempts to capture the timeless original of the Old Masters, Hilda, as copyist, mimics the epistemology of the subject/object dichotomy of modern scientific methodology that, as

original work of the Old Masters, Hilda reveals the Platonism behind her puritanical nature as she denies her own life in history as well as the historical nature of human understanding. Such an epistemology, whether claimed by Hilda or not, enables her own lack of intellectual and emotional engagement with the world.

Hawthorne's evocation of Plato's theory of representation, as demonstrated by his portrayal of Hilda as copyist, suggests Gadamer's critique of Plato's mimetic theory in his own understanding of the nature of art and aesthetic experience.[12] Gadamer argues that, in contrast to Plato, Aristotle's *Poetics* rightly identifies the meaningfulness inherent in our experience of art by pointing to its participatory nature, as is evident in the notion of tragic catharsis. By including the response of the spectator within his definition of tragedy, Gadamer argues, Aristotle describes our experience of art as one of encounter, therefore creating knowledge outside the bounds of the subject/object dichotomy of scientific, or methodological, thinking. Further, Gadamer argues that a proper understanding of the notion of tragic catharsis as a purification of the emotions of pity and fear underscores the nature of the knowledge gained in tragedy. Gadamer explains that the "impure" element in these emotions that Aristotle refers to is, in fact, the disjunction we feel in the face of the dilemma confronting the hero; it is "a refusal to accept" the agonizing events. The effect of the tragic action, or the emotional response—the mix of pleasure and pain—we feel in response to its dramatization, is to remove this disjunction with "what is" or "what exists" (116). It reconciles us to the reality of

---

Gadamer argues, removes the subject from history in order to grasp an object objectively, for the purpose of scientific knowledge and control. Her Platonic understanding of the nature of reality, therefore, prioritizes, at the expense of phenomena and the temporal, an eternal form outside of history, which can be known and apprehended.

[12] Hans-Georg Gadamer, *Truth and Method*, trans. Joel Weinsheimer and Donald G. Marshall (New York: Crossroad, 1991).

what has happened to the hero before us, and, as the hero is exemplary, to what can happen to us as historical, mortal beings. It is, therefore, our common fate that we affirm or recognize in our experience of tragedy, our own finitude. Therefore, Gadamer concludes with Aristotle that what we gain as participants in the aesthetic experience is self-understanding; an encounter with an other—with the world that the work of art represents—is, in fact, a deeper encounter with self. Further, as recognition of human finitude constitutes the essence of this self-understanding, "what is" comes to be understood as "what cannot be done away with" (320), and human knowledge becomes, therefore, understood as radically limited.

It is this understanding of the nature of self and knowledge and the humility that arises from our participation in common history that Hilda sorely lacks. As both artist and person, Hilda fails to achieve the insight into human character and experience that should be the result of our experience of art. In his analysis of the transformational value of art, Gadamer describes the achievement of self-knowledge in a way that mirrors Hawthorne's formulation of romance as a process of self-discovery. Adopting the traditional humanistic term of "Bildung," Gadamer underscores the importance of self-education, or cultivation, as the goal of aesthetic experience and of humanistic endeavor, generally. He cites Hegel's usage of the word to indicate the spiritual or intellectual process of assimilation by means of which one becomes more completely oneself through encounters with an other.[13] "To seek one's own in the alien," Gadamer writes, "to

---

[13] Gadamer traces the linguistic history of the concept of "Bildung" from its origin in medieval mysticism to the later development of the term as used by Kant and Hegel. Kant, he argues, uses the term "Kultur" to refer to the particular cultivation of given talents or skills. Because such a use of the term designates the cultivation of a specific talent aimed at self-improvement, it assumes "an act of freedom by the acting subject." In contrast, Gadamer points out that Hegel's adoption of the term "Bildung," after Kant, restores its original meaning within the mystical tradition. Here, Bildung refers to a

become at home in it, is the basic movement of spirit, whose being is only return to itself from what is other" (15). Self-development is here, then, conceived as a continual process in which a new level of selfhood is achieved, as the self encounters and merges with things outside itself, in the process of its development. This circular structure of Bildung, aimed at reconciliation, therefore, points ultimately to the essential historical nature of human being. Past merges with present, self with other, in a continual present, or creation of living meaning. Against the presumption of modern method, then, which asserts a transcendent subjectivity, Gadamer's dialogic notion of understanding points to reconciliation and relationship, and thus to a recognition of finitude as the essential human situation which the reasoning mind cannot transcend in the hopes of understanding tradition, the self and others, from an idealizing perspective.

The concept of Bildung, then, applied to Hawthorne's novel, suggests that Hilda's approach to painting, and to the moral obligations in life, is wrong and repressive, of herself and of human nature, generally. Hawthorne thus assigns to her the same fate as he does to his other Puritan Innocents whose idealism has failed them. Like Young Goodman Brown, for instance, who loses his faith in "Faith"—and consequently in life—after his evening in the woods, Hilda becomes a cynic who is unable to see any good in the world as she is forced to recognize the reality of evil after her recognition of Miriam's participation in crime. With this "dismal certainty of the existence of evil in the world," Hawthorne

---

state "according to which man carries in his soul the image of God after whom he is fashioned and must cultivate it in himself." Bildung here, then, is seen as the development or aspiration of the whole self toward a universal. In this more "profound" understanding of the term, Gadamer argues, "that by and through which one is formed becomes completely one's own." My point, here, is that Bildung, understood properly as defined by Gadamer, indicates that same continual process of development and assimilation, of reconciliation, by means of which we achieve understanding (*Truth and Method,* 10-15).

writes of her, "it is as if a cloud had ... gathered over the morning light ... the effect is almost as if the sky" has fallen with our friend, "bringing down in chaotic ruin the columns that upheld our faith." [14] We ultimately discover, however—as Hawthorne reminds us of this cynic—that it is not actually the sky that has fallen, "but merely a frail structure of our own rearing, which ... has fallen because we founded it on nothing" (329). As Hawthorne has shown us before, such clear-sighted idealism is not adequate to the task of encountering complicated moral reality.

In this novel about art and art theory, Hawthorne dramatizes Hilda's loss of faith in Miriam—and consequently in the good of the world—by means of her inability to appreciate and idealize the works of the Old Masters as she formerly had. In the chapter, "The Emptiness of Picture-Galleries," Hilda wanders the long galleries and cold marble halls "wondering what had become of the splendour that used to beam upon her from the walls" (341), as she looks for the moral comfort that she now needs and fails to find there. Hawthorne, writing as art critic for Hilda, explains the reason for this failure of her once beloved works of art to speak to the emotional demands of her new experience. He tells us that the painters of the majority of pictures filling the galleries substitute technical merit and "a keen, intellectual perception" for human interest or "live sympathy and sentiment" (338), and that indeed they might "call their doings, 'Art,' for they [had] substituted art instead of Nature" (336). In more good and insightful art criticism, he tells us that the "love of Art ... differs widely in its influence from the love of Nature; whereas, if Art had not strayed away from its legitimate paths and aims, it ought to soften and sweeten the lives of its worshippers"; it ought to "comfort the heart in affliction ..." (340). For Hawthorne, then, art ought to have something to do with life. He consequently writes that while Hilda had not given up "all Art as worthless," the great work of art, in

---

[14] Hawthorne, *The Marble Faun,* 328.

itself, or for its own sake, "had lost its consecration" (341), and Hilda, as a result of her experience, had ceased to be "so perfect a copyist" (375).

What Hilda has lost is the aesthetic sensibility that divorces the work of art from its world, or frees it from the necessity of speaking truthfully about that world, a criterion for artistic merit that Hawthorne and Gadamer hold in common. The reader is, therefore, not surprised to find that the painting Hilda most desires to see, as she wanders the galleries looking for meaning and spiritual consolation, is Sodoma's fresco of Christ bound to a pillar. In a long passage, the tone of which reveals Hawthorne's own appreciation of the work, he describes the effect of this painting on the spectator:

> One of the most striking effects produced, is the sense of loneliness. You behold Christ deserted both in Heaven and earth .... Even in this extremity, however, he is still divine .... He is as much, and as visibly, our Redeemer, there bound, there fainting, and bleeding from the scourge, with the Cross in view, as if he sat on his throne of glory in the heavens! Sodoma, in this matchless picture, has done more towards reconciling the incongruity of Divine Omnipotence and outraged, suffering Humanity, combined in one person, than the theologians ever did. (340)

Having passed, then, "from picture-galleries into dungeon-gloom" and back again (375), Hilda learns to recognize the truth of art, and hence for Hawthorne the criterion for true art, as it speaks meaningfully to our experience of the world. For Hilda, who sees moral reality in dichotomous terms, and has banished her friend because of it, this means that a proper appreciation of art, as well as a right understanding of life, involves a reconciliation of the ideal and the actual, a recognition of the reality of historical being that the painting of the suffering Savior so well exemplifies. Matured by her experience of suffering, she consequently recognizes the "moral enigma" that her friendship to Miriam presents her with, as she thus sets off, at decline of day, to deliver Miriam's package to the Cenci palace.

The circular pattern of Hilda's process of maturation, her encounter, that is, with moral reality outside the self, which leads to a more accurate understanding of self and the nature of human being, points, ultimately, back to the question raised by the notion of the "fortunate fall" that underlies the novel.[15] It is Miriam, as Hawthorne's dark woman, who first articulates the meaning of the fortunate fall to Kenyon as it pertains to Donatello's transformation from a natural creature to a man of thought and feeling. He is now, she notes, "so changed," and yet, "in a deeper sense, so much the same." "Travell[ing] in a circle as all things heavenly and earthly do," he "[has come] back to his original self" immeasurably improved "from [his] experience of pain" (434). While his previous life had been full of happiness, even perfect, it was, as Kenyon notes, "within circumscribed limits" (321); it did not comprehend the full range of human experience and, therefore, was not true to the reality of human nature and existence as Hawthorne has defined it. Similarly, Hilda has undergone such a transformation. While she rejects Kenyon's further speculation regarding the notion of the fortunate fall—claiming that "If there be any such dreadful mixture of good and evil as you affirm ... then the good is turned to poison ... " (384)—she has learned, through her knowledge of Miriam's guilt, the reality of human

---

[15] This question of the fortunate fall has been accepted as a major theme of the novel as early as F. O. Matthiessen's classic study. However, as Millicent Bell and Terence Martin have noted, it is the secularity of the notion of the fortunate fall as voiced by both Miriam and Kenyon—in which salvation comes exclusively through the achievement of human knowledge, not through the grace of God—that complicates the question for Hawthorne. Indeed, as Martin has argued, it is Hilda's acceptance of the fact of Donatello's transformation and simultaneous rejection of the secular version of the fortunate fall that subverts Hawthorne's central theme of transformation.

frailty and the value of compassion. This is made clear, at novel's end, as she contemplates the symbolism inherent in the circular shape of the bracelet that Miriam has given her for a bridal gift. As Hawthorne writes, "And now, happy as Hilda was, the bracelet brought the tears into her eyes, as being, in its entire circle, the symbol of as sad a mystery as any that Miriam had attached to the separate gems. For, what was Miriam's life to be? And where was Donatello?" (462). Donatello, of course, as Hawthorne tells us in the "Postscript," is in jail, having entrusted judgment of his ambiguous crime to human authority, and Miriam seems fated to lonely exile. Hilda, however, as it would appear in this final scene, has learned to value the reality of the sad mystery of life that evades the dichotomies and harsh judgment that she would impose upon it.

The evolution of Hilda's character, then, would suggest that what she has achieved, and what Miriam articulates, is an accurate understanding of the nature of historical being. Hilda's repressive idealism engenders an aesthetic sensibility that interrupts her life as both artist and friend. She refuses, because she feels unworthy, to lend her own authentic voice to the ongoing tradition that is artistic interpretation, and she imposes life-denying either/or categories of understanding onto a complex moral reality. Judging from the fates of his characters, Hawthorne suggests that such a categorical understanding of experience refuses our life in history—does not speak truthfully to the limits we face, as we must answer to the mandates of both head and heart. Against this idealism that Hilda represents, which, as Gadamer warns, often becomes a subjectivism that encroaches on the world, the events of the novel suggest that we understand the nature of understanding rightly. As in the experience of art, our achievement of understanding in life involves an encounter with an other, likewise immersed in history, and, ultimately, allied with self. Knowledge is, therefore, self-knowledge if we acknowledge the claims of history upon us; our experience of the world is properly seen as a circular process of self-discovery, and, therefore, of limit. What Hilda gains, as she moves through the art gallery one last time, suffering from the loss of Miriam's friendship as much as from the knowledge of her friend's guilt, is a right understanding of the nature of both art and life. In her understanding of aesthetic experience as that of encounter, she evolves from a Platonic preoccupation with form to an Aristotelian appreciation of content, and to a tragic recognition of the limitation that is our and Hawthorne's "common nature." If only through the insight granted her by her recognition of emotional loss—both real and represented—she ceases to be "so perfect a copyist" and becomes a better friend.

# 4

# O'CONNOR AS "REALIST OF DISTANCES": ROMANCE, PROPHECY, AND THE MODERN MIND

In terms of both matter and mode of representation, Flannery O'Connor places her narrative art within the context of the American romance tradition. Throughout her letters and the critical essays collected in *Mystery and Manners*, she allies her own aesthetic theory with that of both Hawthorne and Henry James. Citing Hawthorne's well-known definition of the romance in his preface to *The House of the Seven Gables*, O'Connor explains that her artistic interest is in the possible rather than in the probable, "in what we don't understand rather than in what we do" (*MM* 42), and that her intention is to reveal what *can* happen in ordinary life and human experience, not necessarily what does. While all writers are "fundamentally seekers and describers of the real" (49), she argues, their realism will depend upon their own particular vision and the convictions that they hold regarding what they see. For O'Connor, then, as well as for Hawthorne, the mode of representation for the romance writer depends upon a balance of inner and outer worlds or a "neutral territory" between the "actual and imaginary."[1]

O'Connor's interest in what she considers to be the poetic quality of romance lies as much in its vision as in its form. As she

---

[1] Nathaniel Hawthorne, "The Custom House," in *The Scarlet Letter* in vol. 1, *The Centenary Edition of the Works of Nathaniel Hawthorne* (Columbus: Ohio State University Press, 1962) 36.

describes the domain of the romance writer, she distinguishes it from the verisimilitude demanded by realism and from the determinism of literary naturalism. Contrasting the romance with these forms, she writes that her intention is to portray the universe as a mysterious "created order" to whose laws her characters "freely respond," and to render an experience of mystery to her reader (41). As a Christian writer, her emphasis on mystery, freedom, and, indeed, on free will versus determinism, reveals a clear relation between her fiction and the American romance tradition as defined by Hawthorne and as critically formulated by Richard Chase in *The American Novel and Its Tradition,* a study O'Connor knew and admired.[2] As Hawthorne claims the subject of the romance to be not the historical accuracy of social verisimilitude but the "truth of the human heart"[3] Chase defines the romance as a "border" fiction.[4] As such, he explains that it is concerned, if not with the traditional American borderland between town and country, frontier and society, then, with the tension between inner and outer reality, or with the psychological borderland of the human mind. The mimetic aim of the romancer, as such writers of the American romance as Hawthorne, Melville, and Faulkner make clear, is thus not to faithfully describe external reality, but rather to reveal mystery, conflict or contradiction, within the individual.

It is within this tradition of what O'Connor calls the "dark and divisive romance-novel," then, that she places her own work. As O'Connor describes the heroes of her own fiction, they are "forced out" beyond the ordinary and the everyday in order to "meet evil and grace" (*MM* 40, 42); as she has insisted, defending

---

[2] Richard Chase, *The American Novel and Its Tradition* (New York: Gordian, 1957).

[3] Nathaniel Hawthorne, preface to *The House of the Seven Gables* in vol. 2, *The Centenary Edition of the Works of Nathaniel Hawthorne* (Columbus: Ohio State University Press, 1965) vii.

[4] Chase, *The American Novel,* 19.

such grotesques as Hazel Motes, her distorted characterizations have an "inner coherence" that fits the frame of romance, if they do not cohere to a "social framework" or to social expectations (42). Her affinity with the romance tradition is also evident from her many critical statements on the subject of her fiction (46). She writes that "a story always involves, in a dramatic way, the mystery of personality," and consequently, that the subject of good fiction is "human nature" (90, 120). Further, and to the point of the nature of romance, O'Connor explains that she shares Hawthorne's beliefs regarding the nature of human nature. In an interview with Gerard Sherry in the spring of 1963, she states, "I write 'tales' in the sense Hawthorne wrote tales … I'm interested in the old Adam. He just talks southern because I do." [5] As a Catholic, then, O'Connor shares with Hawthorne, if not an institutional affinity, then at least a religious belief in the reality of original sin and the essential dividedness of human nature. Dwelling on paradox and contradiction, the "truth of the human heart" becomes, for O'Connor, "the mystery of personality" (*MM* 90) and existence, generally, and the bedrock of all experience she describes as that of human limitation.

As a Southerner, Flannery O'Connor finds the historical experience of the South to be fit material for romance. In her essay entitled "The Regional Writer," [6] O'Connor quotes Walker Percy when she attributes the prevalence of good Southern writers to the South's loss of "the War." She explains that this does not simply mean "that a lost war makes good subject matter [,]" but rather that the South has experienced its "Fall." "We have gone into the modern world," she continues, explaining Percy's comment, "with

---

[5] Rosemary M. Magee, ed., *Conversations with Flannery O'Connor*, Literary Conversations Series (Jackson: University Press of Mississippi, 1987) 98.

[6] Flannery O'Connor, "The Regional Writer" in *Mystery and Manners: Occasional Prose*, ed. Sally and Robert Fitzgerald (New York: Farrar, Straus and Giroux, 1969).

an inburnt knowledge of human limitations and with a sense of
mystery which could not have developed in our first state of
innocence—as it has not sufficiently developed in the rest of our
country" (*MM* 59). Because of its history of defeat, then, the South
is a "conquered people," as writer Caroline Gordon put it in a
symposium of Southern writers that included O'Connor, and as
such, the Southerner "know[s] something" that writers in other
regions of our rich and democratic nation do not know.[7] Its unique
historical experience has thus engendered within the South a sense
of "poverty," or recognition of the loss O'Connor believes to be
inherent in the human situation, and so interesting and fruitful for
the fiction writer, as he or she deals with the subject of human
nature (*MM* 131).

Interpreting this experience of human loss and fallibility
intrinsic to Southern history is, of course, the Protestant
fundamentalism that pervades the region. O'Connor explains the
importance of the fact of the South as Bible Belt for both the
Southerner and the Southern writer. Defending her own use of the
grotesque and the prevalence of the grotesque in Southern fiction,
in general, O'Connor claims that if Southern writers "have a
penchant for freaks ... it is because we are still able to recognize
one." She continues, "To be able to recognize a freak, you have to
have some conception of the whole man, and in the South the
general conception of man is, still, in the main, theological" (44).
Knowledge of the Bible, she explains, has given Southerners a
moral absolute against which to measure themselves; in the South,
she writes, we have a vision of "Moses as he pulverized our idols"
(59). Thus, in the South, she continues, the Bible is read by
everyone, educated and ignorant alike, and sacred scripture gives
"meaning and dignity to the lives of the poor."[8] The "poor"
O'Connor defines universally as those "afflicted in both mind and
body," and in spirit, and thus, for O'Connor as fiction writer, the

---

[7] Magee, *Conversations,* 66.
[8] Ibid., 83.

"freak" in Southern fiction—a region O'Connor claims to be Christ-haunted if not Christ-centered—becomes a "figure for our essential displacement" (*MM* 44–45).

O'Connor's sense of the finitude fundamental to human nature, and of the mystery that surrounds human existence, rests, ultimately, on her Catholicism. ("The two circumstances that have given character to my own writing have been those of being Southern and being Catholic," she writes [196].) In a well-known statement, she explains that "belief ... is the engine that makes perception operate" (109), and as a writer, she "admit[s] to certain preoccupations" with belief, death, grace, and the devil.[9] Responding to those critics, however, who would suggest that such a fundamentalist belief in Catholic dogma would restrict her vision of the world, censoring, for instance, what she would allow herself to see according to the teachings of the Church, she explains that, on the contrary, Catholic doctrine affects her fiction primarily by guaranteeing her respect for mystery. It provides her with what she calls "the whole gaze," an expanded vision that grounds the concrete and natural in the "eternal and absolute" (*MM* 45, 27), and she attributes her use of the grotesque to its influence:

> My own feeling is that writers who see by the light of their Christian faith will have, in these times, the sharpest eyes for the grotesque, for the perverse, and for the unacceptable ....
> The novelist with Christian concerns will find in modern life distortions which are repugnant to him, and his problem will be to make these appear as distortions to an audience which is used to seeing them as natural. (33)

As this passage makes clear, O'Connor's use of the grotesque has a prophetic function. Contrasting her own use of distortion with the verisimilitude of realism, O'Connor explains that the "realism of [the] novelist will depend upon his view of the

---

[9] Ibid., 103.

ultimate reaches of reality" (40–41), and, further, that "in the novelist's case, prophecy is a matter of seeing far things close up. The poet is a realist of distances, and it is this kind of realism that you find in the best modern instances of the grotesque" (44). Unlike the grotesques of the frontier tradition, then, and of the Southern writers of local color, she explains that though her grotesques may be comic, they are "not primarily so" (44). Rather, they are grotesque "because of a directed intention that way on the part of the author" (40), and as such, they are deadly serious as they are intended to convey or embody the mystery, or poverty, central to human experience. Thus, contrasting the novelist who is an orthodox Christian with the mere naturalist, O'Connor explains that the Christian novelist "lives in a larger universe"; for him or her, the natural contains and suggests the supernatural (175). As she employs the grotesque, then, she explains that, when attempting to communicate to a modern, secular audience for whom only the natural exists and for whom evil is not a mystery, for instance, but only a problem to be solved, her means will have to be that of distortion. She will have to resort to "ever more violent means" to get her message across, to convey the concrete fact of the rite of baptism, for instance, to an audience to whom it is meaningless because it is unnecessary. O'Connor's use of the grotesque as narrative technique, then, rests on a Catholic sacramental vision, as it recognizes the reality of grace and, therefore, of evil and human finitude. As O'Connor herself explains, her Catholic faith assures her sense of mystery and provides her with what she calls "a sense of continuity from the time of Christ."[10]

O'Connor thus contrasts this Catholic sensibility with the modern sensibility that she characterizes in terms of its ration-

---

[10] Ibid., 38.

alism. In her essay entitled "Novelist and Believer," [11] she provides a definition of the modern consciousness that is both characteristic of and definitive for her thought and fiction:

> For the last few centuries, we have lived in a world which has been increasingly convinced that the reaches of reality end very close to the surface, that there is no ultimate divine source ... the popular spirit of each succeeding generation has tended more and more to the view that the mysteries of life will eventually fall before the mind of man. (*MM* 157–58)

Such a rationalistic worldview is, further, subjective, as it privileges the knowing mind over the material world, and, as it assumes an autonomous subjectivity divorced from the world, it is inherently dualistic. O'Connor explains that the dominant characteristic of the modern and secular mind, the root of its rationalism, is the separation of grace and nature. Contrasting the modern worldview with that of the Christian Middle Ages, O'Connor writes that while "St. Augustine wrote that the things of the world pour forth from God in a double way: intellectually into the minds of angels and physically into the world of things," to the modern mind, "there is no ultimate source ... the things of the world do not pour forth from God in a double way, or at all" (157–58). Consequently, as grace has been separated from nature, as the sacred source has been banished from creation, the natural has been devalued and viewed as inherently corrupt. O'Connor writes that the modern world is infected with this Manichean temperament which, as it devalues the material, seeks to transcend it, to avoid entanglement with the world, or with the body, "in an attempt to approach the infinite directly" (168). Such a Manichean temperament, O'Connor notes, contrasting the dualism characteristic of modernity with her own Catholic sacramental

---

[11] Flannery O'Connor, "The Novelist and Believer," in *Mystery and Manners: Occasional Prose*, ed. Sally and Robert Fitzgerald (New York: Farrar, Straus and Giroux, 1969).

vision as writer, is inimical to both the writing of fiction and to our human relationship to the natural world.

As a Catholic writer intent on the revelation of mystery, O'Connor explains that it is the task of the fiction writer to render this experience of "mystery" through "manners." ("There are two qualities that make fiction," she famously writes. "One is the sense of mystery and the other is the sense of manners. You get the manners from the texture of existence that surrounds you" [103]). Throughout her critical writing, she underscores the importance of recognizing the concrete, sensual nature of fiction, or what she calls its "incarnational nature." Accordingly, though her vision of the mystery, and hence finitude, that surrounds human existence, allies her with Hawthorne, her concern for technique, for the proper embodiment of mystery through manners or sense experience, allies her more closely with Henry James. She shares James's criticism of Hawthorne's tendency as writer toward allegory, or toward rational meaning, rather than dramatic, embodied meaning, and indeed, in an interview, has remarked that though she does in fact write "tales" as Hawthorne did, she hopes she does so "with less reliance on allegory."[12] In words that echo James, then, in the ideas they convey if not in idiom, O'Connor warns that the beginning fiction writer must be attentive to the concrete. Employing her characteristically wry wit, she complains that though "the world of the fiction writer is full of matter," beginning writers "are very loath" to bring this world to life. She notes the tendency on the part of new writers to be reformers and idealists and to substitute formula, technique, and theory for people, place, and situation, and comically concludes, "they don't have a story, and they wouldn't be willing to write it if they did..." (*MM* 90–91).

In more serious terms, however, O'Connor laments the consequences to fiction writing of this Manichean sensibility,

---

[12] Magee, *Conversations,* 98.

which, having banished grace, or the sacred, from creation, has likewise resulted in the dissociated sensibility of modernity. For writers infected with this Manichean temper, she explains, "judgment exists in one place and sense-impression in another." The modern Manichean, she continues, even one possessed of a religious consciousness, believing nature and grace to be separated, "attempt[s] to enshrine the mystery without the fact," and there follows a "further set of separations ... inimical to art. Judgment [is] separated from vision ... and reason from imagination" (184). For the writer of good fiction, however, for the one not infected with this fundamental dualism that severs thought from feeling, head from heart, O'Connor explains how "judgment begins in the details he sees and how he sees them" (92). For this writer, "everything has its testing point in the eye, and the eye is an organ that eventually involves the whole personality" (91). She quotes Henry James directly when she explains that "the morality of a piece of fiction depend[s] on the amount of 'felt life' that is in it," that is, what the author feels about, or the judgment that she renders about, what it is that she sees (*MM* 146). For both O'Connor and James, then, judgment is implicit in the act of seeing; thought and feeling are united.

O'Connor's own sense of "felt life"—those assumptions that form the basis of her judgment as she looks at and measures the world—are provided by her Catholic belief. O'Connor draws from St. Thomas as extensively as she refers to Henry James in the formulation of her own theory regarding the integrated sensibility that makes good art. O'Connor explains that St. Thomas called art "reason in making"; "the artist," she explains, "uses his reason to discover an answering reason in everything he sees. For [the artist,] to be reasonable is to find, in the object, in the situation, in the sequence, the spirit which makes it itself" (*MM* 82). "In art," she further explains, "reason goes wherever the imagination goes."[13] Accordingly, then, Catholic Christianity has provided O'Connor with the re-association of sensibilities absent from the modern world.[14] Her belief provides her with the conviction that the universe is meaningful, and, therefore, her reason follows her faith, and her imagination as artist, in bringing forth this meaning. O'Connor expresses these sentiments on the subject in an important letter to Alfred Corn, a college student who had written to her wrestling with questions of faith. In the letter, in which this Thomistic influence is implied, she writes that one of the consequences of "modern liberal Protestantism has been ... to make truth vaguer and vaguer and more and more relative, to banish intellectual distinctions, and to depend on feeling instead of thought." The modern mind, thus, comes ultimately to believe "that God has no power ... and that religion is our own sweet invention." Against this modern dualism that results in subjectivism, O'Connor writes that as a Catholic, she believes "the opposite of all this ... that God has given us reason to use and that it can lead us toward a knowledge of him" (*HB* 479). For the Catholic artist, then, the material world is good and meaningful as it proceeds from a divine source, and it is the prophetic function of the artist to reveal this sacred source. Through the imaginative use of reason, the artist brings to light the meaning perceived by faith. Unlike the modern Manichean, then, for whom nature, as it is corrupt, is only valuable for its utility, for O'Connor, as Catholic artist, the "good," or well-crafted, work of art mimics the good work of creation itself.

As would be expected, the devaluation of the natural or material that results in the writing of what O'Connor considers to be bad fiction has consequences for our human relations as well.

---

[13] Ibid., 233.

[14] This point was first made by Marion Montgomery, who argues that just as O'Connor's critique of the dissociated sensibility has these Catholic roots, her belief provides her with a "reassociation of sensibilities" that recognizes the incarnational or dramatic nature of fiction ("Realist of Distances," 227).

The fundamental dualism that underlies the modern sensibility creates not only what she has called "sorry religious fiction," but also a "sorry," or vague, morality. As grace has been separated from nature, she writes, there is a tendency on the part of the modern dichotomous mind to "compartmentalize the spiritual," to "make it resident in a certain type of life only," and as the supernatural is banished, she further explains, it is "gradually apt to be lost." She thus warns that this Manichean sensibility that bifurcates reality, severing the spiritual from the material, tends to make the religious excessively pious and the natural "obscene." She describes the consequences of this bifurcation as it is evident in the tastes of the "average Catholic reader" who, having reduced his conception of the supernatural to pious cliché, is drawn only to the sentimental, or to the pornographic:

> We lost our innocence in the Fall, and our return to it is through the Redemption ... and by our slow participation in it. Sentimentality is a skipping of this process in its concrete reality and an early arrival at a mock state of innocence .... Pornography, on the other hand, is essentially sentimental, for it leaves out the connection of sex with its hard purpose, and so far disconnects it from its meaning in life as to make it simply an experience for its own sake. (*MM* 147–48)

Such a sentimental experience of nature is symptomatic of a modern subjective sensibility that, having severed grace from nature, is itself divorced from a meaningful relation to reality. There is an assumption of false, or "mock," innocence to such a sensibility, she notes, in which the self is not really held to, or engaged in, nature, the mind not restricted by matter. O'Connor finds such sentimentality and subjectivism, as did Hawthorne before her, to be at the root of our modern notions of progress, as it finds the physical or essential, nature and human nature, to be amenable to mind. Further, because it is based on an act of abstraction, she finds it to be equally inefficacious. As modern humanity has, at best, but "a diluted sense of evil," she explains, modern subjectivism issues in an easy, sentimental compassion. Such compassion, despite the best intentions of the reformer, is ultimately ineffective because, as it refuses to recognize the reality of evil, it does not recognize the root of the problem of suffering. Consequently, she explains, citing the taste of the modern reader as an example of this modern dualism, if the reader looks for grace, "if he believes in grace at all," he or she looks for it as a serving of "Instant Uplift"; he or she fails to affirm the larger sense of compassion, "the sense," she writes, "of being in travail with and for creation in its subjection to vanity," or human pridefulness (166).

O'Connor, ultimately, then, equates the modern liberal sensibility with a subjectivism that negates the reality of the outside world, or reduces it to concept in the name of progress.[15] As grace is separated from nature, the human mind becomes its "own ultimate concern" (159). Thought becomes identified with all of reality, and, as it assumes unmitigated power over nature, secular reason becomes deracinated, or for the Christian believer, cut loose from being itself and the ability to recognize its common divine source. Reality for the deracinated, secular intellect is thus reduced to abstraction. In O'Connor's words, the hero of much modern fiction is, therefore, "the outsider." "His experience is

---

[15] John Desmond has identified this subjectivist slant of the modern consciousness in his sketch of the philosophies of history that have shaped O'Connor's artistic vision and theory of representation. Tracing the roots of the modern consciousness to the early modern or post-Medieval world, he explains that at this time, spanning the Renaissance and Enlightenment, we became aware of our own subjectivity, of ourselves as the "free and active cause of [our] own thought and existence." Human existence became "historically conditioned," as "[e]verything—God, nature, events—seem[ed] capable of being subsumed by the mind ...." Our new "historical con-sciousness" thus gave us unrestricted power over nature (*Risen Sons,* 101). For a recent treatment of O'Connor from the perspective of gnosticism, especially as it pertains to American culture, see Christina Bieber Lake.

rootless. He can go anywhere. He belongs nowhere" (199–200). He or she is thus characterized as an abstractionist who, having banished the sacred from matter, equates matter with mind, and by virtue of autonomous secular reason, is able to transcend, and ultimately to assume power over, creation.

O'Connor's critique of deracinated, or secular, reason has its roots, as Marion Montgomery points out, in a Thomistic philosophy of nature, just as O'Connor's aesthetic theory rests on St. Thomas's premises regarding the making of art.[16] In his three-volume study of the "presumptuous will" of the modern Gnostic or Manichean mind, Montgomery distinguishes the philosophy of St. Thomas on the question, "What is being?" from that of later thinkers who likewise consider the question.[17] He ascribes the banishment of "being" that has been performed by modern subjectivism to the evolution in the priority given to the concepts of *esse* and *ens* that has occurred in the existentialist tradition. Montgomery explains that *esse* (or the being of beings, the ground of all being) takes priority over *ens* (or discrete objects in the physical world) for St. Thomas and thinkers in the Christian tradition. Later atheistic thinkers, however, such as Sartre, prioritize the existence of *ens*, or individual beings, over *esse* as the source of particular things. The atheistic thinkers, therefore, can equate individual objects with their perception of them; they assert their own "imaginative will, " as Montgomery explains of Sartre, against *esse*, as the ground of being or God, and, they thus become the makers of their own world.[18] Existentialists in the tradition of St. Thomas, however, acknowledge that things in the world exist separate from their perceptions; they exist as givens

---

[16] Marion Montgomery, *The Prophetic Poet and the Spirit of the Age*, 3 vols. (La Salle IL: Sugden, 1981–1984) vol. 2, 327–31.

[17] Ibid., vol. 3, 12–14; vol 2., 324.

[18] Ibid., vol. 2, 324–27.

first, if we are able to perceive them at all.[19] As Montgomery points out, O'Connor's characterization of art as "reason in making" (*MM* 82), or her assertion that the artist uses his or her reason "to discover an answering reason" (82) in the created world, therefore assumes that the world has meaning that is intelligible, as Thomas posits.

This important distinction between *esse* and *ens* thus applies to makers of art as well as to those who would apprehend the world philosophically or scientifically. Montgomery explains that as all artists are dependent upon primary creation to supply the material, or the *givens*, of their art, they are creators on a "secondary level" ("Realist of Distances," 271).[20] (O'Connor would, of course, agree as she defines the artist as "realist of distances," intent on revealing the inherent sacrality of creation.) Thus, as Montgomery explains, the poet "does not imitate nature as a mirror imitates the object, but rather imitates the *operations* of nature, that action which may be said constituted by the relation of *esse* and the *ens*." Imitating the "actions of God"—rather than becoming an "imitation god," as moderns have suggested—"the

---

[19] In a helpful gloss on the insights offered by Montgomery, Deal Hudson explains that, similar to atheists writing in the existentialist tradition, those writing in the tradition of Thomistic "existentialism" distinguish between essence (*essentia*) and existence (*esse*), or "between the things that have concrete existence and the essences that exist either as the 'form' of individual substances or as ideas in the mind." The principle of "real distinction," or the priority given existence over essence, means, for the Christian thinkers, that things "must first receive *existence* in some fashion" before they can be "known by another mind." (Similarly, Montgomery notes that "[f]or Thomas, it is the *esse* that is "actual existence" [*Prophetic Poet*, vol. 2, 326].) Thus, while both the Christian and atheistic existentialists prioritize existence over essence, a very important distinction is made ("Marion Montgomery" and 'The Risk of Prophecy'," 243–43).

[20] Marion Montgomery, "Flannery O'Connor: Realist of Distances," in *Realist of Distances: Flannery O'Connor Revisited*, ed. Karl-Heinz Westarp and Jan Nordby Gretlund (Aarhus, Denmark: Aarhus University Press, 1987) 271.

finite" imitates the "infinite perfection." The artist "calls an artifact into being, not *ex nihilo* but *ex esse*."[21] It is the function of the prophetic poet, then, as Montgomery explains in his analysis of O'Connor as such a poet, or as a "realist of distances," to call us back to a recognition of "being" itself, to give the world back its "body," or, as O'Connor would have it, to embody "mystery" through "manners."

This call for a return to "being," or for a recognition of the mystery that lies at the heart of existence, that O'Connor has in common with St. Thomas, recalls Gadamer's assertion of the historicality, or temporality, of human being. In his critique of the subjectivism, and hence dualism, that governs the methodological basis of the modern mind, it will be remembered, he calls for a recognition of this fundamental temporality, or finiteness, of our understanding. While for St. Thomas and the Christian existentialists, the *givenness* of creation, the autonomous, independent existence of the world that is prior to mind, is given by God, for Gadamer, following Heidegger, it is a consequence of the historical condition of our "thrownness," of the fact that we exist in a historical situation of being "thrown" into the world in a certain way, at a certain time, and, thus, are predisposed toward the world in a certain, or particular, way.[22] Thus, assuming the

---

[21] Montgomery, *Prophetic Poet*, vol. 2, 330.

[22] Critics have remarked on O'Connor's affinity with the tradition of phenomenology and existentialism. As Farrell O'Gorman notes, O'Connor's sense of the anxiety and alienation that attends the modern age, and attracted her to such writers as Romano Guardini over traditional Catholic humanists (*Peculiar Crossroads*, 77), establishes common ground with even such atheistic existentialists as Heidegger. His concept of "thrownness" here indicates the radically temporal nature of understanding in a world that lacks a foundation in the absolute. While Heidegger views the temporality of existence as the positive ground for understanding, O'Connor herself was sympathetic to the plight of the unbeliever in the modern world, especially in the aftermath of WWII, when both faith and reason could seem irrelevant. Similarly, O'Connor's insistence on the concrete, experiential nature of art would align her with other such fundamental precepts of existentialism as the

historical nature of existence, Gadamer re-describes the process of understanding in such a way as to move beyond the subject/object dichotomy of scientific method. Because we exist in history, in time, Gadamer writes, we live within tradition that prevents reason from becoming autonomous. There is, therefore, a "belongingness," or essential unity, between self and world. The achievement of understanding is, thus, a relational or reciprocal process, involving dialogue and mutuality, rather than method. Further, to step outside of this dialogic structure, Gadamer warns, in order to know an object objectively, or in itself, is to diminish the independent life of the object, its claim to meaningfulness. Gadamer uses the example of the doctor/patient relationship to underscore the ethical consequences of this pursuit of objectivity. The doctor, he argues, is interested in the patient not as a possible enhancement to his or her own knowledge, but as an object to be known, and consequently diagnosed.[23] The person/patient is reduced for the purpose of diagnosis to a concept that is then understood, and manipulable, by mind. To think ahistorically, Gadamer concludes, to separate knower from known, subject from object, is either to think theologically, in which such a "being-in-itself" is not for human understanding, or it is to think like Lucifer, "as one who would like to prove his own divinity by the fact that the world has to obey him." Such modern methodological thinking therefore assumes the pride inherent in the modern scientistic will-to-power, in which knowledge, Gadamer claims, is "knowledge for domination."[24]

---

priority of existence over essence, and its focus on the historical situation of the individual, rather than on systems, theories, and abstraction. For other discussions of O'Connor and existentialism, see John Sykes, Frederick Asals, and Kathleen Feeley.

[23] Hans-Georg Gadamer, *Truth and Method*, trans. Joel Weinsheimer and Donald G. Marshall (New York: Crossroad, 1991) 270.

[24] Ibid., 406.

O'Connor and Gadamer have in common, then, this critique of modern consciousness as it is characterized by the deracinated intellect or by the subject/object dichotomy of modern method. In O'Connor's fiction, this deracinated intellect is dramatized by her characterizations of the modern rationalist. Such a character would seek to reform or improve material being—nature and human nature—by means of the knowledge of, and hence control over, being granted by sovereign, or detached, reason. While several such rationalists appear in her fiction—Julian in "Everything That Rises Must Converge," Asbury Fox in "The Enduring Chill," and Sheppard in "The Lame Shall Enter First"—her most poignant example is Rayber in *The Violent Bear It Away*. In this second romance-novel, O'Connor places in conflict, through the characterizations of Rayber and Old Tarwater, the secular, autonomous intellect of the rationalist with the prophetic imagination of the "realist of distances," as she has defined it. As she dramatizes this conflict of drives that exists within each of us, she thus reformulates, within Catholic Christian terms, the conflict between head and heart that is characteristic of Hawthorne before her. [25] As Hawthorne's idealists must face the consequences of a hubris that attempts to transcend, and often destroys in the process, material being, Tarwater, the hero of the romance, must choose between "the life of reason and that of prophecy."[26] His ultimate choice thus points to what O'Connor considers the right human relation to being—that is, to one based on recognition of human limitation and hence of empathy with creation, rather than on the destructive force of the autonomous intellect that would remake or mold external reality in its own image.

The story opens with the death of Old Tarwater, a backwoods prophet who has raised his orphaned great-nephew Francis Marion

---

[25] Flannery O'Connor, *The Violent Bear It Away,* in *Collected Works of Flannery O'Connor,* ed. Sally Fitzgerald (New York: Library of America, 1988).

[26] Magee, *Conversations,* 47.

Tarwater to follow in his footsteps. Granted a vision by the Lord, Old Tarwater had rescued young Tarwater from his uncle Rayber, who had wanted to raise him in the city, "according to his own ideas." As narrated by O'Connor, Old Tarwater then fled with the boy to the backwoods where the Lord had told him to "raise him up to justify his Redemption" (*CW* 331). The old man had thus taught him his "History beginning with Adam expelled from the Garden and ... on down through the presidents to Herbert Hoover and on in speculation toward ... the Day of Judgment (331)." As the culmination of this learning, Old Tarwater had schooled the boy in the importance of his "election" as prophet. He tells him that he had saved him "to be free, [to be his] own self." Because of his action in kidnapping the orphaned boy from Rayber, his schoolteacher uncle, Old Tarwater tells him he had been preserved from a conventional upbringing and a traditional schooling where he would have been "indistinguishable," "one among many" (339, 341). "While other children his age were herded together in a room to cut out paper pumpkins under the direction of a woman," Old Tarwater explains, "he was left free for the pursuit of wisdom ..." (340). The old man further explains, in an attempt impress upon the young man the importance of his election to prophecy, that he had been saved from the "ideas" of the schoolteacher, from being inside the schoolteacher's head, nothing more than "a piece of information," "laid out in parts and numbers" (341).

Early on in the novel, Old Tarwater identifies Rayber as an abstractionist and a rationalist. He explains to the boy, and to the reader, that he had first gone to live with Rayber on "Charity," but had soon "found out [that it] was not Charity or anything like it" (331). Under the pretense of genuine interest, Old Tarwater explains, Rayber had crept "into his soul by the back door, asking him questions that meant more than one thing, planting traps around the house and watching him fall into them" (331). While the old man reports that Rayber had seemed delighted "to talk about the things that interested him," all that this interest bore were "dead words" (341). Instead, Rayber had composed a diagnostic study of Old Tarwater for a psychology journal. "Where he wanted me was inside that schoolteacher magazine," Old Tarwater explains. "He thought once he got me in there, I'd be as good as inside his head and done for and that would be that, that would be the end of it" (342). In her own narrative voice, O'Connor describes this interest of Rayber in Old Tarwater as that of the objectifying process of scientific investigation, in which "living thing," as she explains, becomes "concept":

> The schoolteacher's house had little in it but books and papers. The old man had not known when he went there to live that every living thing that passed through the nephew's eyes into his head was turned by his brain into a book or a paper or a chart. The schoolteacher had appeared to have a great interest in his being a prophet, chosen by the Lord, and had asked numerous questions, the answers to which he had sometimes scratched down on a pad, his little eyes lighting every now and then as if in some discovery. (341)

Rayber, as scholar/scientist, studies his uncle as prophet in order to offer a diagnosis. Explaining his prophecy—that which Rayber, as rationalist, considers to be his madness—he writes in the journal article that "[t]his fixation of being called by the Lord had its origin in insecurity. He needed the assurance of a call and so he called himself" (378). He further refers to his uncle as a "type," whom "[t]ime has passed by" (339, 376)—his choice of language here revealing his modern temperament, his predisposition toward progress based in reason. O'Connor's passage of description of Rayber in his first encounter with the younger Tarwater underscores the rationalism that characterizes him as a diagnostician. As he answers Tarwater's summoning knock, O'Connor writes that he came to the door

> plugging something into his ear. He had thrust on the black-rimmed glasses and he was sticking a metal box into the

waist-band of his pajamas. This was joined by a cord to the plug in his ear. For an instant the boy had the thought that his head ran by electricity .... The boy found himself scrutinized by two small drill-like eyes set in the depths of twin glass caverns .... Already he felt his privacy imperiled. (386)

This description, of course, recalls Hawthorne's own scientist/scholars—his Chillingworth, Aylmer, Ethan Brand—and O'Connor's intention in her characterization of Rayber is to reformulate the tendency toward abstraction and the objectification of being characteristic of the idealist/reformer who would remake the world according to his own image. While Hawthorne's characterizations rest on a critique of the detached or isolated intellect of the scientific sensibility, generally, however, O'Connor's Catholic Christian reformulation of the fundamental dichotomy rests specifically on a critique of the modern consciousness as it is characterized by the deracinated intellect, or by that intellect that, since the modern era, has equated thought with reality and thus freed itself from the necessity of engagement with creation. Therefore, Hawthorne's scientist/idealists become O'Connor's secular reformers, intent on transforming the world for good as the ability to do so lies within the domain of reason. Accordingly, Rayber is characterized by the Enlightenment rationalism that informs his idealism as a reformer. In comic passages near the beginning of the novel, he impresses upon Tarwater the need for a good education so that he may assume his place in the world as an "intelligent man" (399). He introduces him to the trappings of civilization, to museums and art galleries, to air travel as "the greatest engineering achievement of man" (438). Most important to O'Connor's critique of Rayber's rational idealism, however, as these secular notions of self-improvement suggest, is the religious significance that it assumes. As Rayber explains to Tarwater, the only way for humankind to "save" itself is the "natural" way, by means of its own "intelligence" (45). Believing Tarwater to be the victim of a compulsion in his drive to baptize Bishop, then,

Rayber asserts himself as "savior" to Tarwater as he had to his uncle before him. As he explains to Tarwater, "You need to be saved right here now from the old man and everything he stands for. And I'm the one who can save you" (438). Believing, as he states, that this compulsion can be understood "for the good reason that it [is] understandable," Rayber claims that he will "lift the compulsion from [the boy's] mind, expose it to the light, and let him have a good look at it" (446).

The religious significance of Rayber's rationalism is dramatically underscored in an important passage in the novel in which, having followed Tarwater—who has gone into an Evangelical temple—Rayber listens at the window to the young girl who is preaching to the crowd. As he listens, O'Connor writes, he feels pity for "all exploited children—himself when he was a child, Tarwater exploited by the old man, this child exploited by parents, Bishop exploited by the very fact he was alive" (412). Moved by his pity, and responding to her narration of the story of the Lord saving the Christ-child from Herod, Rayber envisions himself playing the part of "an avenging angel," moving "through the world ... gathering up all the children that the Lord, [as he believes] not Herod, had slain" (413). As O'Connor notes, he envisions "himself fleeing with [this] child to some enclosed garden where he would teach her the truth, where he would gather all the exploited children of the world and let the sunshine flood their minds" (414).

As this passage suggests, Rayber's rationalism, his belief in his ability to reform the world and to transcend human imperfection and suffering, issues in the false or mock innocence that O'Connor describes as intrinsic to the modern sensibility. Such a false innocence, it will be remembered, results from a dichotomous vision that, having banished grace from nature, reduces mystery to problem, and is, therefore, confident in the ability of reason to eliminate suffering. Such idealism, however, as the fate of Rayber and also of Hawthorne's Aylmer and the community at Blithedale make clear, is naïve and doomed to failure as it does not take seriously the reality of evil as the root of suffering. As O'Connor has argued, such idealism often results in a sentimental view of life that, as it is unrealistic about the reality of evil, often ends in bitterness. Thus, it will be remembered that Rayber's pity for the child preacher is also self-pity for his own past suffering. He remarks to Old Tarwater, as an instance of this self-pity, that, having abducted him from a loveless home and having told him of the love of Christ for him, Old Tarwater had "ruined [his] life," had filled him with "idiot hopes" and "foolish violence" (376–77), and he explains that the "calamity" of the old man's abduction of him was that he "believed him." "For five or six years," Rayber explains, "I had nothing else but that. I waited on the Lord Jesus. I thought I'd been born again and that everything was going to be different or was different already because the Lord Jesus had a great interest in me" (436). Thus, when Old Tarwater explains to young Tarwater that he had "planted the seed" of faith in Rayber and that it "was there for good," he rightly understands the hope—that which O'Connor calls the "inherited tendency to mystical love" of creation—he has awakened in Rayber as a human being of heart as well as of head (*CW* 373, *HB* 484).

Rayber's intuitive tendency to love—the heart that must balance his head—is represented, of course, by his love for his son Bishop. As Rayber knows, although he tries to think of the boy as "part of a simple equation," "an *x* signifying the general hideous-ness of fate," at times, "with little or no warning, he would feel himself overwhelmed by ... love" for him:

Anything he looked at too long could bring it on. Bishop did not have to be around. It could be a stick or a stone, the line of a shadow, the absurd old man's walk of a starling crossing the sidewalk. If, without thinking, he lent himself to it, he would feel suddenly a morbid surge of the love that terrified him—

powerful enough to throw him to the ground in an act of idiot praise. It was completely irrational and abnormal. (401)

Bishop thus serves Rayber as the focal point for what he considers his "hated" and "horrifying" love of creation itself, "the curse," he explains, "that lay in his blood" (401). Ironically, while this overwhelming love begins with Bishop, it also ends there. Without the boy's presence, O'Connor notes, Rayber would be given over to this unconditional and irrational love; "the whole world would become his idiot child" (442). The mentally retarded Bishop, then—with white hair, pink face, and clear and bottomless eyes— serves O'Connor as an obvious symbol of the inherent sacrality of creation, of a creation that is good in itself, as it manifests its divine origin. As the dim-witted child with "knobby forehead" and sunken eyes mirrors the divine (349), Rayber's involuntary love for him reveals his own love of creation itself. Accordingly, as an enlightened man of reason, Rayber's response to this love is to deny it. Not looking at "anything too long," and sleeping "in a narrow iron bed," he deprives his heart and his senses. Balanced "between madness and emptiness," O'Connor writes that he intends to "fall on the side of his choice" (402), to maintain what he, as rational unbeliever, considers his dignity. Choosing mind over matter, then, stifling his love for Bishop as it symbolizes his love for creation and Christ, he subordinates heart to head in an effort not to feel the pain of love for, and hence the possibility of the loss of, the creation of which he is a part.

O'Connor's characterization of Rayber's rationalism is important for the contrast that it provides with the character of Old Tarwater. In an interview with Joel Wells in 1962, O'Connor defines the central conflict of the novel as the clash of these two personalities. The "great Uncle," she writes, "is the Christian—a sort of crypto-Catholic—and … the school teacher … is the typi- cal modern man. The boy … has to choose which one, which way, he wants to follow."[27] O'Connor's description of Old Tarwater as a "crypto-Catholic" is the significant distinction between him and Rayber. Though as a Fundamentalist Protestant, Old Tarwater "lacks the visible Church [,] … Christ is the center of his life,"[28] as O'Connor explains, and faith, therefore, provides him with the imaginative vision characteristic of the prophet. Thus, while his antics may appear comic and literalistic at times—he insists that Tarwater place a cross at the grave "to show [he's] there" when the crosses are gathered (*CW* 338)—his actions express a belief, as O'Connor explains, in "the … fundamental doctrines of sin and redemption and judgment" (*HB* 350). Such doctrines, as O'Connor reminds us, preserve the mystery of God's grace and entail recognition of the sacrality of creation as it manifests its divine source. As "crypto-Catholic," then, Old Tarwater's prophetic imagination provides him with a sacramental sense of creation that is markedly distinct from the modern dichotomous vision of Rayber. In a letter to Betty Hester, O'Connor further elucidates her criticism of Rayber's dualism when she makes the important point that Rayber's rationalism is that of the "Atheist of Protestant descent" (*HB* 141). Understood in these terms, his atheism stems from what she has described as the Manichean sensibility of the modern mind, that dualistic vision that would separate grace from nature, and that characterizes Protestantism. (As she writes to her friend Dr. T. R. Spivey, the Protestant temper attempts to approach the "spiritual directly instead of through matter" [304].) Lacking a sacramental sense of creation, such a Manichean temper tends to devalue the material world, or values it only in terms of its utility, as is evident in Rayber's behavior. Not only, for instance, does he do for Tarwater all that he would do for Bishop "if it were any use" (*CW* 389), but at the old man's death, he quickly reduces the forest surrounding Powderhead to "probable board feet into a college education for the boy" (444–45). As is evident by

---

[27] Ibid., 88.
[28] Ibid., 83.

O'Connor's comments regarding the central conflict of the novel, Tarwater must choose between these two modes of being toward the created world. His character embodies both the potential for the prophetic imagination of his great-uncle as well as the modern secular mind of Rayber. At the death of Old Tarwater, O'Connor notes, fearing "the threat of the Lord's call (*HB* 350)," Tarwater escapes to the city and to his schoolteacher uncle; the story thus centers on the assertion of his own will against the will of the Lord as it is manifest in his call to prophecy.

In her characterization of Tarwater's struggle, O'Connor dramatizes another aspect of the modern consciousness: Raised by a prophet for prophecy, Tarwater has images of this calling that are the predictably romantic ones of a fourteen-year-old boy. Thus, as he admires the "bedraggled and hungry" image of his great-uncle, who returns from the woods after having made "his peace with the Lord," he respects the old man's romantic freedom and thinks he looks the way "a prophet ought to look" (334). When Old Tarwater reminds him, however, of the meaning of this freedom in Christian terms, that he was "born into bondage and baptized into freedom, into the death of the Lord," Tarwater grows bored and defiant. As O'Connor writes, at these times the boy "would feel a sullenness creeping over him, a slow warm rising resentment that this freedom had to be connected with Jesus and that Jesus had to be the Lord" (342). Thus, while Tarwater's romantic musing and resentment of authority, whether of that of Christ or of his great-uncle, serves O'Connor comically in her characterization of him as an adolescent, it further introduces the possibility of his unbelief and the assertion of individual will that will likewise serve her metaphorically. As Rayber dramatizes the modern rationalist, whose reason would usurp the place of the divine, O'Connor's characterization of Tarwater indicates the modern existentialist who, believing the cosmos to lack meaning and moral authority, asserts his individual will in an effort to create his own truth and destiny.[29] As an example of modern, secular humanity, then, Tarwater is characterized as an unbeliever who, nevertheless, in his drive to baptize Bishop, fears the call of the Lord. As such, as he is torn between his vocation as prophet and his own desire to defy ultimate religious meaning, he dramatizes the conflict between belief and unbelief that, for O'Connor, characterizes the modern sensibility.[30]

Throughout her narration of Tarwater's story, O'Connor dramatizes the urgency and the ethical consequences of this conflict for modern humanity. Referring to the imagery of the cross that is associated with him throughout the novel, she writes in a letter to John Hawkes that Tarwater is one who is "marked out for the Lord," or, at least, as one who "will have the struggle, who will know what the choice is" (*HB* 350). In this same letter, she defines this choice, recalling the words of the Misfit in "A Good Man Is Hard to Find":

> " [Jesus] thown everything off balance," [the Misfit explains.] "If He did what he said, then there's nothing to do but thow away everything and follow Him, and if He didn't, then it's nothing for you to do but enjoy the few minutes you got left the best way you can—by killing somebody or ... doing some other meanness to him.'" (*CW* 152, *HB* 350)

As O'Connor makes clear, however, in her characterization of this killer, one cannot choose "nothing" as one of the terms posed by this existentialist dichotomy. In a world in which no objective moral absolute is posited, to choose to believe in nothing is to choose evil, as morality is thus reduced to subjectivism, to individual choice and the assertion of individual will, and hence of

---

[29] For a full discussion of Tarwater as existentialist, see Jane Keller.

[30] In a letter to John Hawkes, dated September 1959, O'Connor writes of *The Violent Bear It Away* that we "breathe in with the air of the times" this conflict "between an attraction for the Holy and the disbelief in it" that characterizes the novel (*HB* 349).

the will-to-power.[31] Thus, the Misfit concludes, regarding his decision to dispatch the grandmother for her religious conventionalism, her hypocrisy, and silliness, "She would of been a good woman ... if it had been somebody there to shoot her every minute of her life" (*CW* 153).

In *The Violent Bear It Away*, the ethical implications of nihilism are dramatized in a dialogue between Tarwater and the "stranger," a voice that inhabits Tarwater's mind immediately after the death of his great-uncle, when he is first faced with the responsibility of his new freedom:

> The way I see it, [the stranger says], you can do one of two things.... You can do one thing or you can do the opposite.
>
> Jesus or the devil, the boy said.
>
> No, no, no, the stranger said, there ain't no such thing as a devil.... It ain't Jesus or the devil. It's Jesus or *you*. (354)

Tarwater's freedom dramatizes the assertion of the will of the individual against any objectively determined moral absolute. As such, it issues in subjectivism that further results in a moral relativism that has evil consequences. O'Connor herself speaks to the amorality inherent in nihilism in a well-known passage from a letter to Hester. The "moral sense," she explains,

> has been bred out of certain sections of the population, like the wings have been bred off certain chickens to produce more white meat on them. This is a generation of wingless chickens, which I suppose is what Nietzsche meant when he said God was dead. (*HB* 90)

---

[31] Ralph Wood makes a similar point regarding the nature of nihilism when he applies the words of Dostoevsky's Ivan Karamazov—"If God is dead, all things are permitted"—to his discussion of the Misfit ("Modern Nihilism").

In her folksy language, O'Connor here suggests that the modern subjective sensibility will recast reality—as the Misfit shows as he dispatches the grandmother—in order to fit its own schemes of meaning and justice, to meet its own purposes.[32]

In *The Violent Bear It Away*, the "stranger" thus asks Tarwater his own version of the question Pilate poses to Christ in John 18:38: "What is truth?" The "stranger" asks, "How do you know if there was an Adam or if Jesus eased your situation any when He redeemed you?" "And as for Judgment Day ... every day is Judgment Day" (*CW* 359). Toward the end of the story, Tarwater himself makes clear the ethical consequences of his nihilism. Understanding his freedom, in existentialist terms, as a necessary assertion of will, he believes that he must drown Bishop in order to avoid baptizing him. As he explains to the woman at the Cherokee Lodge: "You can't just say NO .... You got to do NO .... You got to show you mean it by doing it. You got to show you're not going to do one thing by doing another. You got to make an end of it" (427–28).

The significance for the story of Tarwater's struggle, of course, lies in his inability to escape belief, and, hence, in his final determination of a right relation to being. Despite his assertion that he will not baptize Bishop, he understands, as O'Connor writes of their first encounter, "with a certainty sunk in despair, that he was expected to baptize the child," that it was his destiny to trudge

---

[32] For a full discussion of Nietzsche and nihilism, see Henry Edmondson. He notes the progression, pertinent to O'Connor's thinking, from the Enlightenment belief in reason and human goodness to the doctrine of human perfectibility and Nietzsche's "overman," as it is grounded in the need to free humankind from the "bankrupt" philosophies of religion and tradition (*Return to Good and Evil*, 19-20). See also Wood's discussion of the historical onset of nihilism. While, like Nietzsche, O'Connor saw the demise of the Judeo-Christian God as the partial fault of the Church itself, Wood notes that her response, following Romano Guardini, was to cling to the Church as the only refuge against what would become a culture of death (*O'Connor and the Christ-Haunted South*).

"into the distance in the bleeding stinking mad shadow of Jesus..."
(387–88). O'Connor characterizes Tarwater, then, as she did Hazel
Motes, hero of *Wise Blood* before him, as "Christ-haunted."
(Images of crucifixion run through the novel. His face appears as
"cross-shaped," pains of hunger and thirst shoot down and across
him.) Thus, though O'Connor writes specifically of Motes and the
conflict of wills between belief and disbelief that characterizes
him, her comments apply equally to Tarwater when she explains
that his "integrity ... lie[s] in what he is not able to do" (*MM* 115).
Tarwater, like Motes, as an example of modern humanity, is not
able to deny his hunger for Christ and hence for meaning.

Tarwater's predicament, then—the images of crucifixion, the
unfathomable and nauseating hunger, that characterize him in his
struggle against belief—points to what O'Connor believes is the
absurdity of the existentialist position as manifestation of the
modern consciousness, that one can simply will away what one
chooses not to believe. Hence, Tarwater, as existentialist, but also
as Everyman, dignified and free, must "answer for his freedom"
(*CW* 467). Accordingly, as he asserts what O'Connor calls his
"selfish will" against the will of God (*HB* 387), that is, as he
drowns Bishop, he likewise utters the words of baptism, and thus
loses the struggle. As he returns home, having suffered the
indignity of a rape and humbled now into recognizing the reality
of evil, O'Connor grants him a final vision. Looking out over the
field that surrounds his home, she writes that "[i]t seemed to him
no longer empty but peopled with a multitude" all being fed "from
a single basket." As he spies the old man in the crowd, watching
for the approaching basket, the boy leans forward, too, "aware at
last of the object of his hunger, aware that it was the same as the
old man's and that nothing on earth would fill him" (478). As
these images suggest—and as O'Connor herself claims—the novel
is a "minor hymn to the Eucharist" (*HB* 387). As Tarwater, early
in the novel, had denied the sacrality of creation, turning his eyes
from particular things—"a spade, a hoe, the mule's hind quarters

before his plow, the red furrow under him"—fearing that he would be asked to name them "and name [them] justly and be judged for the name he gave [them]" (343), his final vision indicates that he has become the prophet he was intended to be. As such, he has become a "realist of distances." Rid of the dichotomous vision of modernity, which would divorce grace from nature, and, hence, assuming the death of God, would further reduce morality to subjective will, he understands the inherent sacrality of creation and his responsibility to "[the children of God]." Thus, the burning bush for which he had been waiting, his sign, his commandment to prophecy, appears finally as a "red-gold tree of fire" (478), consumed, as it happens, by the fire he has just set to clear the ground of the "stranger," the voice of modern nihilism.

# 5

# GIVING FLIGHT TO "WINGLESS CHICKENS":
# ART AS THE "ADDED DIMENSION"

In her "*Introduction* to A Memoir of Mary Ann," Flannery O'Connor makes a startling statement regarding the nature of compassion. Regarding the loss of religious faith in the modern world, she writes that we now "govern by tenderness," and that tenderness detached from its source results in "terror," in "forced labor camps and the fumes of the gas chamber."[1] In the paragraphs that precede this statement, O'Connor remarks that the Aylmers present in Hawthorne's fictional world have multiplied. While Aylmer in Hawthorne's short story, "The Birth-mark," removes the birthmark from his wife's cheek so she is no longer marred by "earthly imperfection," and, in the process, kills her, the modern Manichean, O'Connor fears, destroys the "raw material of good" in order to achieve an image of ideal perfection (*MM* 227). As grace has been banished from nature, the modern rational mind assumes an autonomy that is destructive to the created world. Against this dualism that has resulted in subjectivism, O'Connor asserts her own sacramental vision that insists on the fundamental finiteness of human knowledge. Mystery must not be separated from manners nor judgment from vision. As a writer, she explains that art requires a delicate adjustment of the inner and outer worlds, and she calls upon the "neutral territory" provided by Hawthorne's formulation of the romance in order to convey her

---

[1] Flannery O'Connor, "*Introduction* to A Memoir of Mary Ann," in *Mystery and Manners: Occasional Prose,* ed. Sally and Robert Fitzgerald (New York: Farrar, Straus and Giroux, 1969) 227.

vision to the modern secular audience. As argued in previous chapters, the romance genre embraces mystery rather than factuality; characters are brought to a recognition of their own finitude, and as the genre of romance rightly asserts the independence of the work of art from reality, the reader herself undergoes an encounter that transcends her own subjectivity and results in an experience of mystery and, hence, finiteness. For O'Connor as a Catholic, character and reader each undergo a conversion in which the achievement of self-knowledge results in a discovery of fallen human nature.

"The Artificial Nigger" is one such story that clearly delineates the process of initiation fundamental to the romance tradition as well as to O'Connor's own use of it to meet her Catholic needs.[2] In this story, O'Connor utilizes Hawthorne's "neutral territory" in ways that call upon the events of "Young Goodman Brown." In that story, it will be remembered, Hawthorne's young hero returns to his village after an evening spent in the woods, where he believes he has seen his townspeople and his beloved wife, Faith, similarly engaged in their own evil adventures. Inferring the universality of sin from the presence of his townspeople, Brown becomes a confirmed Puritan on his return to town, unable to participate in town life, and convinced of the total depravity of the human heart. Hawthorne's intermingling of fact and fancy in this story, however, the dark and dusky woods and vague sights and sounds, point to the unreality of Brown's perception, magnified by Hawthorne's assertion that Brown had perhaps dreamt the whole thing. By calling into question the credibility of Brown's Puritan conviction, Hawthorne points to the inadequacy of the Puritans' dichotomous vision to address the divided nature of the human self.

In O'Connor's own story of initiation into the knowledge of divided human nature, "The Artificial Nigger," she similarly

---

[2] ———, "The Artificial Nigger," in *The Collected Works*, ed. Sally Fitzgerald (New York: Library of America, 1988).

examines the inadequacy of Manichean theology to address the complexity of human nature. Here, Mr. Head awakens in the middle of the night to see the majestic moonlight flooding the room as he anticipates the coming of day when he can take his grandson Nelson to the city in order to lead him on a "moral mission" (*CW* 211). While many scholars have noted the parallels between O'Connor's story of initiation and Dante's *Divine Comedy*, the dramatic appearance of moonlight in the first paragraph, as well as O'Connor's demonstrated knowledge of Hawthorne's stories, essays, and notebooks, suggests an explicit connection to elements of the romance.[3] Just as Goodman Brown's perception is called into question in Hawthorne's tale, the moonlight in this story's first paragraph—indeed in the first sentence—undermines Mr. Head's perception and the credibility of his moral vision. As the narrator blends the real and the imaginary, imbuing floorboards with the color of silver, transforming "ticking" on his pillow into brocade, an ironic distance is drawn between the "dignifying light" of the moon cast on the surroundings and the meager reality of the furnishings of Mr. Head's room.[4] The straight chair looks "stiff and attentive" as if awaiting an order; Mr. Head's trousers, hung over the back of the chair, have a "noble air, like the garment some great man had just flung to his servant." Indeed the "miraculous moonlight" bestows on Mr. Head's tubular face and rounded open jaw the "look of composure" and "ancient wisdom ... of the great guides of men."

---

[3] See, for instance, William Rodney Allen ("Mr. Head and Hawthorne"). His study of "The Artificial Nigger" as romance links the use of moonlight in the story to the transformative effect of moonlight in Hawthorne's "The Custom House." Edward Strickland also discusses O'Connor's short story in terms of the quest romance as defined in Northrop Frye's *The Secular Scripture*.

[4] Louis Rubin was the first to call attention to the comic effect of the mock-heroic tone of the opening scene in his discussion of the literary qualities of the story in contrast to the dominant religious approaches to O'Connor's fiction.

"The only dark spot in the room," O'Connor writes, "was Nelson's pallet, underneath the shadow of the window" (*CW* 210). Nelson will continually act as a foil to Mr. Head's majestic and magnified self-regard, as he undermines the ability of this provincial country innocent to carry out the moral education of his grandson.

In this story, then, rich in comic and symbolic detail, O'Connor reveals the essence of the education to be a contest of wills between an old man and a boy, who appear to be the double of each other. (Mr. Head, she writes, "had a youthful expression by daylight, while the boy's look was ancient" [212]). The story ends with their undoing as each is brought to a recognition of human suffering and sinfulness, demonstrated first by the grandfather's betrayal of Nelson and universalized by their recognition of the suffering conveyed by the statue of the artificial nigger. Just as narrative and verbal irony consistently call into question Mr. Head's intellectual and emotional maturity, the locus of their feelings of superiority lies in their attitudes about race. Mr. Head taunts Nelson about his visit to the city, saying, "It'll be full of niggers" (212). He taunts Nelson on the train when he is unable to recognize as a "nigger" the huge and majestic coffee-colored man who passes down the aisle of the train. Again, the feelings of racial superiority emanating from the Heads are comically undercut by O'Connor when the black waiters in the dining car are allowed to condescend to these two white innocents. The symbolic use of the color "black" continues to evolve as Mr. Head introduces Nelson to the city's sewer system. The sewer appears to Nelson as a symbolic hell, where, his grandfather tells him, he could be "sucked along down endless pitchblack tunnels" (220). As the story nears its climax, however, the significance of race as catalyst intensifies as Nelson is drawn to the "large colored woman" from whom he asks directions (222). His eyes travel up and over her as he desires to be picked up by her and to "look down and down into her eyes while she held him tighter and tighter. He had never had such a feeling before. He felt as if he were reeling down through a pitchblack tunnel" (223). Black forms move up, half consciously, as he sleeps, and indeed, after Mr. Head has betrayed him, as Nelson walks mechanically behind his grandfather, he feels "a black mysterious form reach up as if it would melt his frozen vision in one hot grasp" (228). The indication here is that Nelson's meeting of the black woman—in a life lived without women—has softened him somewhat and has unsettled him in a way that enables him to begin to feel a hint of forgiveness toward his grandfather.[5] The blackness of the racial other has been transformed by O'Connor into an encounter with the mysterious otherness of the woman who has begun to undermine Nelson's previous self-assuredness.

The transformation of her characters is indicated, of course, by their reactions to the statue of the artificial nigger, the emblem of suffering that points to their own "common defeat" (230). As Mr. Head and Nelson stand looking at the statue, O'Connor writes that they could feel it dissolving their differences like an action of mercy. In the penultimate paragraph of the story—after this climactic encounter with the statue—O'Connor describes Mr. Head's feelings:

> He stood appalled, judging himself with the thoroughness of God, while the action of mercy covered his pride like a flame and consumed it .... He realized that he was forgiven for sins from the beginning of time, when he had conceived in his own heart the sin of Adam, until the present, when he had denied poor Nelson. He saw that no sin was too monstrous for

---

[5] O'Connor herself makes the observation that not only has Nelson "never seen a nigger but he didn't know any women." She, therefore, intends that "such a black mountain of maternity would give him the required shock to start those black forms moving up from his unconscious" (*CW* 931). Gender as well as race, then, combine to displace Nelson from his former concept of self that has been formed only by his experience as a white male raised in an all-male household.

him to claim as his own, and since God loved in proportion as
He forgave, felt ready at that instant to enter Paradise. (231)

In this story of the initiation of Mr. Head into the knowledge
of his fallen nature, O'Connor thus undermines the perception of
her protagonist as she follows Hawthorne in her use of elements of
romance. While Hawthorne's story of Young Goodman Brown
uses irony to undermine the Calvinistic vision of his young hero,
O'Connor's story, from her Catholic perspective, points beyond
Puritan and Protestant Manicheism toward her own incarnational
theology. While Mr. Head recognizes his "true depravity" in
rejecting his own kin, God's mercy overshadows his sin; due to
the Redemption, he feels ready "to enter Paradise." For O'Connor,
then, this acceptance of the mystery of Redemption points to the
reality of original sin, but as grace appears here ready to smother
Mr. Head's "pride like a flame," it also points to the inherent
goodness of creation. As O'Connor states elsewhere, the Christian
doctrine of the Redemption indicates that, for all its horror, God
found human life to be worth dying for (*MM* 146). Her
sacramental vision dramatized here thus undermines the
Manichean sense of the depravity of matter as it asserts the
paradox of Christian mystery: in recognition of our fundamental
dependency on the divine, we are capable of being remade and
perfected.

As I demonstrated earlier, O'Connor puts this sacramental
sense in stark opposition to the modern Manichean mindset that,
as she asserts throughout her fiction and nonfiction, values nature
only in terms of use or its potential for improvement. In "The
Lame Shall Enter First," O'Connor re-formulates another important Hawthorne story, "The Birth-mark," in a way that underscores
the theological roots of her own critique of modern dualism. In
this story of the aspiring 18<sup>th</sup>-century scientist Aylmer who
successfully removes his wife's birthmark, only to end up killing
her, Hawthorne's critique of the egoism that motivates Aylmer's
scientific idealism is clear. However, as Asals has convincingly

argued, Aylmer's failure can be read as a tragic one.[6] Indeed, as Hawthorne indicates in the story, it was not uncommon in this age of burgeoning scientific discovery, for the love of science to rival the love of woman. While Aylmer prepares to remove his wife's imperfection, he understands the risk to her life that he is assuming, yet, as a young scientist, he seems prepared to assume that risk. His efforts at perfection are thwarted by the unfortunate reality of earthly imperfection; the composite man consists of the "spirit *burthened* with clay" (49 [emphasis added]).

In O'Connor's story no such ambivalence exists. As she describes in her "*Introduction* to A Memoir of Mary Ann," "the Aylmers of Hawthorne's fiction have multiplied; busy cutting down imperfection they are making headway also on the raw material of the good" (*MM* 227). The aspiration to redeem matter through rationalism is a result of the sentimentality of modernity. O'Connor's story, then, in contrast to Hawthorne's, rests on her belief in the reality of the doctrines of the Fall and the Redemption, as demonstrated by her characterization of her lead character, Sheppard. We first meet Sheppard as he sits at the kitchen counter eating cold cereal from an individual box, while his son Norton rummages for ingredients such as peanut butter and ketchup to moisten the stale chocolate cake that serves him for a breakfast. The character of Rufus is introduced as Sheppard explains to Norton that he has seen Rufus, who's been released from the reformatory, rummaging through trashcans for food. Sheppard hopes to bring Rufus into his own home in order to help Rufus to improve himself, to achieve his highest potential by means of his high intelligence. As has been remarked by O'Connor scholars, this late story is a reformulation of the story of *The Violent Bear It Away*, with some significant differences.[7]

---

[6] Frederick Asals, "Hawthorne, Mary Ann, and 'The Lame Shall Enter First,'" *Flannery O'Connor Bulletin* 2 (1973): 15.

[7] See, for instance, Asals. He notes that drafts of the manuscript of the novel indicate that among the differences are the appearance of a "Rufus

Unlike Rayber, in the novel, who is not given the opportunity for Redemption by O'Connor (at the death of his son, it will be remembered, he is not able to feel sorrow or remorse), Sheppard is given a final revelation of his own corruption, and by implication, of his dependency on God through his loss of Norton.[8] Similarly, as Feeley has suggested, O'Connor seems to extend compassion to all three characters in the story.[9] Thus, while Sheppard's name and his "narrow brush halo" of white hair are obvious and parodic references to the perverted Christ-like role he'll play in the story, his prematurely white hair also indicates the loss he has been burdened with; his "pink sensitive face" indicates his compassion, though misplaced. Similarly, Rufus's moral outrage regarding Sheppard's belief that he can "save" Rufus from his delinquency through his efforts as counselor resounds with credibility for the reader of O'Connor's letters and essays who recognizes Rufus as the truth teller and bearer of the doctrine of original sin. Finally, the victim of Sheppard's misjudgment is not the inert symbol of the divinity of creation that Bishop was in O'Connor's second novel, but is, instead, the ten-year-old boy grieving the loss of his mother. O'Connor thus reworks familiar themes through characterizations that are more complex and that may, therefore, make her subject of Redemption more meaningful for the reader.

---

Florida Johnson" in the novel who "lacks the pervasive religiosity" of Johnson in the story, and the absence from the drafts of the novel of the story's two dominant symbols: the telescope and clubfoot ("Hawthorne," 4–5).

[8] O'Connor remarks that in denying his love for Bishop, Rayber makes the "Satanic choice" (*HB* 484). As he cuts himself off from his love for his mentally retarded son, denying in him the divine image he intuitively sees, he chooses between his own will-to-power over an imperfect creation and the will of God that we love one another within our common limits. O'Connor's strong feelings here probably justify her unusually harsh treatment of Rayber that many critics have noted.

[9] Kathleen Feeley, *Flannery O'Connor: Voice of the Peacock* (New Brunswick NJ: Rutgers University Press, 1972) 82.

Sheppard's belief that he can "save" Rufus, of course, rests on Rufus's 140 IQ. Because of Rufus's intelligence, Sheppard—as secular humanist and City Recreational Director—believes he can re-create Rufus, through rationalism. He will adopt Rufus as his own, and with counseling, reach through "to the boy in the black caverns of his psyche" (*CW* 622). He will, as he says to Rufus (who has described the source of his delinquency as "Satan"), "explain [his] explanation" to him (601). He will talk with him in his office at the reformatory, a narrow closet he compares with a confessional, except that he doesn't "absolve" (599). Like Rayber before him, Sheppard preaches the miracles of modern science to his young student. He buys Rufus a telescope to penetrate the vast mysteries of space, and a microscope and slides to reveal the "infinitesimal" when "immensity" fails to impress him (617). With the new orthopedic shoe, he will correct the boy's deformed foot, fitting him with a "new spine" (621). With intelligence, Sheppard believes, anything is possible.

Rufus, though, proves a painful foil to all of Sheppard's efforts and beliefs. While Sheppard believes that anger over his clubfoot motivates Rufus's delinquency, Rufus constantly asserts that Satan has him in his power, and he reminds Sheppard that he, himself, is also in Satan's grip. Rufus boldly keeps his foot within sight of Sheppard and refuses to wear the new shoe that Sheppard orders for him. In this story, as it reworks the head and heart conflict of Hawthorne's works as well as the religious themes of O'Connor's second novel, Rufus, like Tarwater, is the corrective to the limited vision provided by Sheppard's rationalism. He asserts the fundamental reality of his own deformity, and his intractable evil reveals the limits of Sheppard's own compassion. (Sheppard comes to hate the shoe, as well as the boy, as his own efforts fail.) Understanding the theological roots of Sheppard's misguided efforts, he exclaims, it "don't matter if he's good, he ain't right!" (604). Good works cannot save an inherently corrupt nature.

In this story, in a way similar to the novel, symbols conspire to point out the inadequacy of the Manichean mindset that informs O'Connor's secular humanists. The ugly, swollen foot is a clear indicator of the reality of original sin; the black, shiny, weapon-like shoe that Sheppard orders indicates the methodical means by which Sheppard, as intellectual thug, will try to reform Rufus. Undermining Sheppard's optimism and faith in reason is O'Connor's vivid description of the interior of the brace shop:

> The brace shop was a small concrete warehouse lined and stacked with the equipment of affliction. Wheel chairs and walkers covered most of the floor. The walls were hung with every kind of crutch and brace. Artificial limbs were stacked on the shelves, legs and arms and hands, claws and hooks, straps and human harnesses and unidentifiable instruments for unnamed deformities. (620)

Set against this imagery of tools of reform is the appearance of Rufus's shoe, as Rufus sits in the chair to be fitted for its replacement. "What was roughly the toes," O'Connor writes, "had broken open again and he had patched it with a piece of canvas; another place he had patched with what appeared to be the tongue of the original shoe. The two sides were laced with twine" (620). As the grotesque imagery indicates, Rufus appears ready to live with his deformity. As violent bearer of the gospel truth, then, he points up Sheppard's corruption to the reader before Sheppard's own final revelation. In the final scene of the story when taunted by the reporter to name the nature of the "suggestions" that Sheppard has made to him, Rufus rightly asserts a spiritual sin, rather than a sin of the flesh. "'He's a dirty atheist,' [Rufus] Johnson said. 'He said there wasn't no hell.'" Sheppard is named by Rufus, then, as a "big Tin Jesus." He lacks substance as he lacks knowledge of spiritual realities, such as the corruption of the flesh and the need for Redemption (630). Interestingly, his Manichean mindset is underscored in an important earlier passage when Sheppard first takes Rufus into his home to begin his project of reform. On their first night together, Sheppard is startled to find Norton hiding in the closet inside his mother's winter coat; he "winces," O'Connor writes, as though he had just seen "the larva inside a cocoon" (607). The image indicates that just as he recoils from this sight of his aggrieved child, he rejects—in a way that will recall Hulga Hopewell of "Good Country People"—his own loss, loneliness, and vulnerability. Sheppard will discover his loss at story's end when his encounter with Rufus, as emissary of evil (so evil as to desecrate the undergarments of the child's dead mother in a sexually charged metaphor), will put him in touch with his own corrupt nature. As he loses Norton, who's been convinced by Rufus that his mother is still literally alive in heaven, Sheppard is granted by O'Connor the revelation of his own selfishness that may become the seed for his salvation.

Sheppard's recognition of his own nature, the finitude and fallibility that, for O'Connor, will necessitate our understanding that the Redemption comes through Christ rather than through the reason that Sheppard embodies, brings to mind another Hawthorne sketch, "The Celestial Rail-road."[10] In this story, Hawthorne parodies the idealism of the Transcendentalists in a piece that is a satire of Bunyan's *Pilgrim's Progress*. In this retelling of Bunyan's tale, the modern pilgrims travel easily by rail over the traditional pitfalls of the Christian pilgrim's journey. The celestial railroad glides easily over the Slough of Despond, filled in now with books of French philosophy, German rationalism, and "essays of modern clergy" (187). The Valley of the Shadow of Death, once so fearsome to the former pilgrims, has been similarly transformed; gas lamps shine radiantly out of the "fiery and sulphurous curse" that pervades the place (194). The cavern Bunyan had described as the mouth of the infernal region has been

---

[10] Nathaniel Hawthorne, "The Celestial Rail-road," in *Mosses from an Old Manse* in vol. 10, *The Centenary Edition of the Works of Nathaniel Hawthorne* (Columbus: Ohio State University Press, 1974).

identified as a "half-extinct volcano," used now to manufacture railroad iron. Indeed, the guide informs the skeptical narrator that Hell "has not even a metaphorical existence" (194). Reaching the end of the Valley of the Shadow of Death, the modern pilgrims come to the former cave of Bunyan's enemy giants, Pope and Pagan, now inhabited by the equally formidable "Giant Transcendentalist" (197). The pilgrims arrive at last to the "land of Beulah," an artificial Eden, where they await entrance at the city gates (204). Their guide, Mr. Smooth-it-away, does not accompany them, having no interest himself in admission to the actual Celestial City.

This brief sketch, then, taken together with Hawthorne's "The Birth-mark," indicates the evolution in theme that will result in O'Connor's "The Lame Shall Enter First." Set against the clubfoot is the telescope, which, like Hawthorne's railroad, will take the reader into a "Celestial City" in which all mystery falls before the eyes of modern humanity. The realities of despair and death have been paved over, and as both the "happy preacher" and Sheppard would proclaim, "Hell has not even a metaphorical reality." Norton's death, however, precipitated by his father's egoism, reveals the foolhardiness behind such efforts. The telescope that opens the heavens for the intellect of Rufus launches Norton's own flight into space as the "space man" that he at last becomes. Regarding Sheppard's interest in space travel, Rufus proclaims: "Those space ships ain't going to do you any good unless you believe in Jesus" (*CW* 627); "I ain't going to the moon and get there alive" (611). The only way to get to paradise is through the Redemption, which Rufus and Norton both understand. "The Lame Shall Enter First" thus underscores the inadequacy of the idealism of the Transcendentalists of Hawthorne's sketch that denies matter to aspire to pure spirit. Such Manicheism will eventually result in the piety and sentimentalism that characterize the modern mind. This is expressed by O'Connor in a notorious passage in which she forecasts the results of Emerson's quarrel with the Eucharist:

> When Emerson decided, in 1832, that he could no longer celebrate the Lord's Supper unless the bread and wine were removed, an important step in the vaporization of religion in America was taken, and the spirit of that step has continued apace. When the physical fact is separated from the spiritual reality, the dissolution of belief is eventually inevitable. (*MM* 161–62)

Against the optimism of Emerson's idealism, O'Connor asserts the sacramentalism of her own vision and will dramatize the consequences of the deracinated intellect that has been set free from the constraints of matter. In *Wise Blood*, O'Connor's first romance-novel, she explores the characteristic dualism of the modern mind as it assumes the form of nihilism; here, her young hero will be shown the limits of his rationalism and the need for grace to redeem an imperfect humanity. His story illustrates, early on, the theme that will become the subject of all of O'Connor's fiction.

As the story opens, we meet Hazel Motes, often referred to as Haze, traveling to the city by train in an attempt to escape his fundamentalist background. From his grandfather—"a waspish old man" who carries "Jesus in his head like a stinger" (*CW* 9–10)— and from his stern and pious mother, Haze has inherited the image of a wrathful God that has instilled in him both a pervasive sense of his own corruption and a fear of death. He feels that if he can avoid evil, he can escape the figure of Jesus who haunts him. Indeed, he commits his first act of penance by walking in shoes filled with rocks in answer to his mother who asks, "'What you seen?' ... 'Jesus died to redeem you'"—as the result of Haze's having seen the naked woman in the coffin at the carnival (*CW* 36). Called to the army, he is confident in his ability to avoid temptation and to return home to Eastrod "clean," to follow in his grandfather's footsteps by leading the life of an itinerant preacher. Once enlisted, however, he is told by his army buddies that he need not worry about being "clean," as he has no soul, and he's pleased that he can get rid of his soul without corruption, that he can be "converted to nothing instead of to evil" (12). Thus, the first step toward transformation is made by O'Connor in this story of a young man's struggle with belief. Returning from the army to Eastrod, Haze finds the town deserted, the basis of his fundamentalist faith razed, and he sets off, rootless, to the city to begin his journey to prove the nonexistence of his soul, and, thus, the lack of need for a Redeemer.

On the train, O'Connor makes the terms of Haze's conflict clear. While he declares mockingly to Mrs. Wally Bee Hitchcock and to the women in the dining car,"'Do you think I believe in Jesus?' ... 'Well I wouldn't even if He existed. Even if He was on this train'" (6–7), his new suit and stiff new black hat are the costume of a country preacher. His pale visage stares back at him out of the dark train window, and he appears nervous, about to jump out of the window one minute while staring down the aisle toward the end of the car the next. Indeed, after attempting to talk with a porter whom he believes is from Eastrod, O'Connor writes that Haze appears "as if he were held by a rope caught in the middle of his back and attached to the train ceiling" (5). He seems hamstrung by his conflict, and the memories of the burials of his family members become Haze's own coffin imagery; he wakes in fear that the top of the berth is closing down upon him, and he calls to the porter to get him out: "'I can't be closed up in this thing!' ... 'Jesus,'" Haze mutters in his fear, to which the porter responds, "Jesus been a long time gone" (14). Dramatic imagery and dialogue thus underscore what appears to be an irresolvable conflict, and Haze will attempt to prove his new doctrine of nihilism by escaping his fundamentalist past.

Upon Haze's arrival in Taulkinham, the bifurcated world that O'Connor warns against becomes apparent. "The black sky," she writes, "was underpinned with long silver streaks that looked like scaffolding and depth on depth behind it were thousands of stars that all seemed to be moving very slowly as if they were about some vast construction work." "No one was paying any attention to the sky," she continues, as the residents of Taulkinham were distracted by the city lights, the signs, and lit storefronts (19). As has been often remarked, the story is pervaded by images that portray people in purely animal terms. On his first night in town Haze visits Mrs. Watts, a prostitute, whose mouth, O'Connor writes, "split in a wide full grin that showed her teeth. They were small and pointed and speckled with green" (18). In another scene, her grin is described as "curved and sharp as the blade of a sickle" (34). She appears dangerous, even predatory, as she asks Haze if he's "huntin' something?" and tells him to make himself at home (18). Everywhere in Taulkinham the spirit seems banished from the flesh, such as when Haze first meets Enoch Emery—his future disciple—at the display of a man selling potato peelers, his pyramid of boxes appearing as an "altar" for the eager buyers of this modern tool. In fact, it is also here that Haze first meets up with Asa Hawks, the fake blind preacher, and his child, Sabbath Lily Hawks, who cuts into the line of the salesman's customers. Hawks knows his audience and which terms to use to appeal to them for money: "Help a blind preacher. If you won't repent, give up a nickel. I can use it as good as you. Help a blind unemployed preacher. Wouldn't you rather have me beg than preach? Come on and give a nickel if you won't repent" (21).

When Haze follows the preacher and his daughter to a domed civic building, Hawks comments that "a program is letting out," and that the crowd is his "congregation" (29). This encounter with the blind preacher—a petty con man who has faked blindness to collect money—underscores the sincerity of Haze's own quest. While the preacher enlists Haze's help, asking him to go to the top of the stairs and "Repent! … Renounce your sins and distribute these tracts to the people," Haze's own earnestness becomes apparent. "I don't believe in sin," he tells Hawks. "Nothing matters but that Jesus don't exist" (29). His renunciation of Redemption is made clear in his first sermon to the Taulkinham crowd:

> Maybe you think you're not clean because you don't believe. Well you are clean, let me tell you that … if you think it's because of Jesus Christ Crucified you're wrong. Don't I have eyes in my head? Am I a blind man? Listen here, … I'm going to preach a new church—the church of truth without Jesus Christ Crucified. (31)

Urging his new doctrine of self-sufficiency, he aptly remarks to Hawks and Enoch, "I don't need Jesus … I got Leora Watts" (31). As Johansen and others have pointed out, Haze's involvement with Leora Watts is his first attempt to prove the nonexistence of sin and his first step in his journey toward self-knowledge.[11]

The secular values of the modern desacralized world are underscored through O'Connor's characterization of Haze's disciple Enoch Emery. While the natural backdrop of Taulkinham—the scaffolding that underpins the sky above it— suggests Haze's struggle against belief, Enoch is completely at home in the city, though as O'Connor makes clear, he's been unable to make friends during the entire two months that he's been there. As a guard at the zoo, he has established himself at "the heart of the city" (*CW* 45). Similarly, he displays a "fondness for supermarkets" and an enthusiasm for the goods of the potato peeler salesman that align him with the secular values and commercialism that the city represents. As critics have noted, his identification with the city allows him, as a foil to Haze, to perform a perversion of the religious quest Haze is undertaking.

---

[11] Ruthann Knechel Johansen, *The Narrative Secret of Flannery O'Connor: The Trickster as Interpreter* (Tuscaloosa: University of Alabama Press, 1994) 119.

His daily ritual after leaving guard duty resembles an inverted "stations of the cross" (Martin 68). He visits the swimming pool where, hidden in the abelia bushes, he spies on what he considers to be near naked women swimming. He visits the FROSTY BOTTLE, where he consumes a chocolate malted milkshake and makes lewd suggestions to the waitress, "whom he considers to be secretly in love with him" (46). His next stop is to visit the zoo animals held in cages that resemble the "Alcatraz Penitentiary in the movies." Animal imagery and images of entrapment allow O'Connor to develop a very important theme in these events that suggest the perversion of a religious quest. In a scene in which Enoch is rushing Haze through his rituals in order to get him to the "new jesus," Enoch, regarding the underside of an ape, remarks maliciously, "If I had a ass like that ... I'd sit on it" (53). While critics such as William Rodney Allen have rightly interpreted this statement as indicative of Enoch's own identification with the purely animal and material world,[12] the remark further indicates O'Connor's ongoing critique of the destructive attitude of the modern deracinated mind in its relation to the created world. In the preceding sentence, O'Connor has pointed to the innocence of the animal, describing the "small pink seat" on the otherwise gray monkey. O'Connor's subsequent reference to Enoch's "prudish" remark further underscores his distance from, and devaluation of, the body that has resulted from its loss of sacramentality. Similarly, Enoch's attitude toward women is purely sexual, and his remarks abusive, as indicated by his comments to the waitress at the FROSTY BOTTLE. Revealing a Manichean attitude toward sex, as it has been severed from its natural function of reproduction, Enoch is a voyeur who merely spies on women at the pool. Indeed, in one scene in which he recognizes Hazel Motes, who has come to the pool to find him, O'Connor writes that Enoch emerges from his spying place within the bushes "on

---

[12] William Rodney Allen, "The Cage of Matter: The World as Zoo in Flannery O'Connor's *Wise Blood*," *American Literature* 58 (1986): 267.

all fours," appearing as an animal (47). In her characterization of Enoch's antics, O'Connor thus dramatizes the consequences of the deracinated intellect that she similarly describes in her "*Introduction* to A Memoir of Mary Ann" in a discussion of the nature of Christian compassion. Just as she writes that "[t]enderness cut off from its source" becomes its opposite in "terror" (*MM* 227), transcendence from the devalued flesh has become "prudishness," and as would be predicted, Enoch's tastes lie in the merely sentimental and pornographic.

This bifurcation and subsequent devaluation of matter is clearly indicated, of course, in O'Connor's narration of the furnishings in Enoch's room. He occupies the "head" of the boarding house in his upstairs room; the washstand that will become the tabernacle to hold the new jesus stands on "bird legs" that have "clawed feet." The "tabernacle-like cabinet" that will house the new Eucharist is actually meant to hold a slop-jar, and the whole furnishing itself is crowned with an overwrought "trellis-work of hearts, scrolls and flowers" and adorned finally "just at the level of Enoch's face" with a small mirror in which Enoch can see his own reflection (*CW* 74). The pictures in the room further comically underscore the debased matter and mock innocence that Enoch is identified with. A picture of a moose "standing in a small lake" adorns one wall. This image of animal innocence is so irritating to Enoch that he removes its frame, as if it were its clothes, in order to humiliate the moose and then places a calendar picture of a "woman wearing a tire" opposite the moose that it is therefore forced to look at. Enoch's favorite picture, we are told, is of a little boy in "Doctor Denton's," kneeling by his bed, praying that God will "bless his daddy" (75). Considering Enoch's own relationship with his abusive father, O'Connor's underscoring of the sentimentality is clear.

While Enoch's compulsion and identification with animality suggest, in Cartesian terms, an emphasis on the merely mechanical and material that is a result of modern bifurcated reality, Onnie Jay

121

Holy serves as a representative of the modern secular and sentimental church.[13] Looking to make a quick buck, he sings the praises of the "Prophet" Haze to the crowd Haze is speaking to. A preacher and radio star, Holy advises Haze of the means by which Haze can make his new church palatable to the modern audience. He thus serves a saccharine version of church doctrine. The Holy Church of Christ without Christ, Holy says—misstating the name of Haze's own doctrine of nihilism—is based solely on the Bible, on one's own personal interpretation. No dogma or doctrine conveys mystery that its believers "don't understand and approve of." "This church is up-to-date!" Onnie Jay assures his audience, "nothing or nobody" is ahead of them (86–87). Holy further explains that the doctrine of Haze's church is based in the "sweetness" of the human soul, the "natural" goodness that life's pressures, "cares and troubles," can drive inside (85). The human person thus becomes mean, and, therefore, lonesome, driven to despair, suicide, and even murder. What is needed, claims Holy, wishing he had his guitar, is a reminder of our natural sweetness that will stave off our lonesomeness, which is at the heart of all evil. In a parody of Romantic belief in natural goodness and self-reliance, Holy speaks in a "sad nasal voice," though smiling all the while, so that his congregation "could tell he had been through what he was talking about and come out on top" (85).

Against Enoch and Onnie Jay Holy, then, O'Connor posits Hazel Motes as her Protestant Saint. Her young hero, as representative of the modern age, will suffer modernity's characteristic conflict. As she writes in a letter to John Hawkes,

---

[13] Henry Edmondson notes O'Connor's "opinion that the troubles of the modern world find their origin in the philosophical revolution introduced by the mathematician and philosopher Rene Descartes" (*Return to Good and Evil,* 84). He attributes the modern bifurcation of reality—the split between reason and faith—to the "hyperrationalist philosophy" of Descartes that will eventually result in the complete subjectification of reality and in nihilism (16). For further discussions of Cartesian elements in O'Connor's fiction, see also Christina Bieber Lake and Frederick Asals.

his will be a struggle against disbelief, against the nihilism that she believes is "the gas [we] breathe" in with the air of modern times (*CW* 1107, 949). Unlike her secular humanists and atheists who have either deified themselves, or learned to "live with despair," Haze, whose name suggests an obstacle to clear perception, is a seeker. He is one who "can neither believe nor contain himself in unbelief" and, as he suffers modernity's characteristic malady, he therefore searches, "feeling about in all experience for the lost god" (*MM* 150). In her preface to the second edition of the novel, O'Connor champions Haze's conflict, crediting him for the integrity that lies in what he is ultimately not able to do as an agent with free will, as he is not able to deny Christ. In this important first novel, his romance thus involves a journey toward self-definition, or as O'Connor has written, toward knowledge of the self that is severed from God's grace.

Haze's effort to evade the faith of his childhood, in an age in which the absolute has been banished, is dramatized by O'Connor's characterization of him as an itinerant. Having returned from the army to find Eastrod deserted, he packs his Bible and his mother's glasses and embarks on his journey to the city to engage in sin and in blasphemy, and, as he implies to Mrs. Hitchcock, to prove his newly found faith in nihilism: If evil does not exist, then sin is meaningless. Once in Taulkinham, his nihilism develops into his doctrine of the Church without Christ that will preach salvation based in self-reliance. The dominant symbol of Haze's secular faith in modern rationalism and empiricism as the source of his mobility and progress is, of course, his Essex. In an important scene, Haze jumps onto the hood of his car, and his preaching makes clear the symbolic significance of his automobile as the source of his newly found freedom from the past:

> I preach there are all kinds of truth, your truth and somebody else's, but behind all of them, there's only one truth and that is that there's no truth ... No truth behind all truth is what I and

this church preach! Where you come from is gone, where you thought you were going to never was there, and where you are is no good unless you can get away from it. Where is there a place for you to be? ... In yourself right now is all the place you've got. (*CW* 93)

The car provides Haze with "a place to be that [he] can always get away in" (65). Like Hester Prynne, who similarly believed in the ability to escape the past in order to "begin all anew," the car—described by O'Connor as a "rat-colored automobile"—will serve Haze as a vehicle of self-renewal. As it carries him about to preach his new doctrine of the Church without Christ, the car, like Rayber's airplanes and Sheppard's telescopes, embodies Haze's faith in the ideals of the Enlightenment, his faith in progress based in reason. "[N]obody with a good car need[s] to worry about anything," he tells the garage attendant; his car "ain't been built by a bunch of foreigners or niggers or one-arm men ..." It was built by people with their eyes open that knew where they were at" (72). Ironically, the car—as symbol of the promise of the Enlightenment—keeps breaking down. It develops a "tic" every day by nightfall; Haze, as an inexperienced driver shoots backwards when he means to go forward; the car has leaks in the radiator, the gas tank, and a leaking tire. The car, as a product of the intellect and will of the modern scientific mind, like his unproductive sex with Mrs. Watts, provides evidence that modern humanity cannot achieve transcendence by its own efforts.

As Kathleen Feeley has pointed out, Haze's transformation involves a series of stages.[14] Haze's sincere confusion over Sabbath's question of whether a bastard can be saved in the new Church without Christ, serves him an early reminder of the contradiction inherent in his doctrine; if there's only one truth, his church, not the Church of Christ, must profess it. While Haze asserts to Sabbath that the word "Bastard" will have no meaning in

---

[14] Feeley, *Voice of the Peacock,* 63.

his church, where "everything is all one," he senses a contradiction: "The thing in his mind said that the truth didn't contradict itself and that a bastard couldn't be saved in the Church Without Christ. He decided he would forget it, that it was not important" (*CW* 69). Secondly, while Haze feels that by murdering Solace Layfield he has rightly rid the world of a false prophet—of someone who doesn't speak "true"—he still bends to hear the words of the dying man, despite himself, thus hearing Layfield's true profession of faith as he confesses to his Christian God. Finally, the destruction of Haze's car leaves him, literally, with no place else to go. To Feeley's observations I would add one more instance of impending revelation, such as the moment of encounter with the new jesus in the museum that presages Haze's growing awareness of the end result of his quest. In a scene that anticipates Nelson and Mr. Head's awakening at the sight of the artificial nigger, O'Connor shows Enoch and Haze bent over the shrunken mummy in the glass case. Describing a portentous moment, O'Connor writes: "All [Enoch] could tell was that Hazel Motes's eyes were on the shrunken man. He was bent forward so that his face was reflected on the glass top of the case. The reflection was pale and the eyes were like two clean bullet holes" (56). As Enoch hears the approach of the bikini-clad woman and her children who had followed them into the museum, he notes: "Hazel Motes had not raised his eyes once from the shrunken man." Moments later, the obscene woman's grinning face appears reflected from the glass with Haze's, and her two children's faces appear "as pans set on either side to catch the grins that overflowed from her" (56). Given readers' understanding of O'Connor as a Catholic writer, it is hard to miss this imagery that suggests Haze's balking, however unconsciously, at the perversion of the doctrine of the real presence, the possible mishandling of the Eucharist.

When the new jesus finally does appear to Haze with Sabbath in their apartment, he understands exactly what the consequences of his secular belief will be. Wearing his mother's glasses that he had brought from Eastrod, Haze sees the mummy as Sabbath and the new jesus approach him; the mummy's face is "partly mashed ... his eyelid ... split" (104). Haze grabs the dead and shriveled body, the empty "skin," and throws it out the back door, the symbolic abyss that the landlady had told him had once been filled by a fire escape when he rented his room in the lodging place of Asa and Sabbath Lily Hawks. The destruction of the mummy—the dead and dried emblem of unredeemed humanity in whom Sabbath sympathetically sees "something of everyone ... as if they had all been rolled into one person and killed and shrunk and dried"—brings Hazel one step closer to his final attempt to flee and his inability to do so (104). O'Connor's use of Haze's mother's glasses here and Haze's ironic assertion that he's "seen the only truth there is" suggest the correction to his vision that is soon to come. After his killing of Solace Layfield—running him down with the Essex—and his attempt to flee to another city, he is stopped by a policeman and his car is destroyed. Admitting to the police officer that he wasn't "going anywhere," O'Connor, in the final chapter, brings Haze to the end of his journey.

O'Connor ends the novel with the interaction of Haze and Mrs. Flood. Mrs. Flood's characterization serves O'Connor by underscoring the meaningfulness of Haze's conflict for the reader, in much the same way that Mrs. Wally Bee Hitchcock did at the story's opening. Mrs. Flood, the landlady, represents the secular values that Haze has successfully escaped. Convinced that he is cheating her, she is determined to keep him around to follow the money trail provided by his government checks. Seeing things in the clear light of day, Mrs. Flood's secular puritan values provide a foil to Haze's own religious awakening. She stares into his blind eyes, scrutinizing them, to find what it is that is being hidden from her. Similar to Ruby Turpin who will come much later in O'Connor's canon, Mrs. Flood believes in class status and is happy to receive his government money—her tax money—that would otherwise go to all the "worthless pockets in the world," to "foreign niggers and a-rabs," "blind fools" and idiots (120). As secular puritan and proprietor of her own boarding house, she counts worth in terms of money, or the "ability to pay," and is scandalized by Haze's backward, penitential behavior that she feels belongs in a "monkery." She tells Haze that she's as good "not believing in Jesus as a many a one that does," and takes as a compliment Haze's ironic words that she is, in fact, "better." "If you believed in Jesus," he tells her, "you wouldn't be so good." Similarly, regarding his penitence of walking with rocks and broken glass in his shoes, she wonders, "Who's he doing this for?" "What's he getting out of ... it?" (125). Clear-sighted and literal, Mrs. Flood displays her pragmatic values when she tells him that time moves forward, not backward, and that there is nobody to help them, but each other: "The world is a empty place." "If we don't help each other ... there's nobody to help us" (128). Ironically, as critics as early as Carter Martin and Feeley have pointed out, Mrs. Flood is granted the beginnings of a conversion.[15] Haunted by the darkness that she perceives behind Haze's eyes, she closes her eyes over his dead face. No longer searching what she believes "had cheated her," she perceives a distant pinpoint of light and follows Haze "farther and farther away, ... into the darkness until he was the pin point of light." A conventional character has followed Haze to the threshold of mystery; she "felt as if she had finally got to the beginning of something she couldn't begin" (*CW* 131).

This awakening to the possibility of eternity on the part of Mrs. Flood has led critics to argue that in this thoroughly Manichean tale in which Haze escapes disbelief only through death, Mrs. Flood, as the one who is left alive, is really the one

---

[15] Carter Martin, *The True Country: Themes in the Fiction of Flannery O'Connor* (Kingsport TN: Vanderbilt University Press, 1968) 120, and Feeley, *Voice of the Peacock*, 58.

who undergoes the beginnings of a conversion.[16] However, described by O'Connor as a Protestant saint, it seems that Haze himself as hero of the novel achieves transcendence within the bounds O'Connor has set for him. If his Protestant belief does not ultimately allow for the indwelling of spirit in matter, if Haze is not able to perceive the presence of grace in the natural world, he does achieve transcendence through his belief in the Christian God who has redeemed him, as he has come to recognize his

---

[16] Asals debates the terms of salvation offered by O'Connor's novel. He argues that by the end of the novel, the split between spirit and flesh is absolute; Haze's "otherworldliness" is posed against Mrs. Flood's materialism and "earthliness." He argues that the two poles prove "irreconcilable." "The grisly comic victory of Hazel Motes is to escape from this world, to mortify his body and seek out death" (*Extremity* 55, 56). The alternative to death, Asals writes, is unacceptable; Haze has the "spiritual integrity" to escape the "secularized worldliness" of Mrs. Flood (55, 56). Marshall Bruce Gentry is much more generous in his treatment of Mrs. Flood and the theme of Redemption, generally. Unlike Asals who finds no possibility for Redemption in the novel, Gentry employs Bakhtin's notion of the positive grotesque to indicate a spiritual rebirth on Haze's part. As Haze chooses death, he argues, he simultaneously chooses to join his deceased family members in "a community of souls whose dead bodies suggest spiritual wholeness" (*Religion of the Grotesque,* 133). The positive grotesque operates in a similar way for Mrs. Flood. Gentry notes that Mrs. Flood "uses her materialism" to eventually understand what Haze is "paying" for, and further, that the image of Haze as a "pinpoint of light" may ultimately serve as an ideal for which Mrs. Flood may strive (135–36). Robert Brinkmeyer applies Bakhtin's notions of dialogic art and the dialogic imagination to treat the issue of Redemption. He argues that Haze's Manichean renunciation of "the here and now" —that Asals has found so thoroughgoing—is undercut as O'Connor's "Catholic vision" competes with the dominant fundamentalist vision of the narrator. While Haze becomes a "fundamentalist saint in his renunciation of the world for Christ," he argues, "Mrs. Flood becomes his follower through Christian charity" (*Art and Vision of Flannery O'Connor,* 114). The very structure of the novel supports Flood's growing charity against the fundamentalism of Haze, for, as he notes," it is Mrs. Flood's story as much as Haze's that ends the book, and it is she who survives and whose vision we last see" (115).

dependence on that God. The reality of his Redemption is borne out by his interaction with Mrs. Flood in the final chapter. As primarily a comic character, her pragmatism and clear-sightedness point out the failure of Haze's earnest and intelligent rationalism. To her protestations that his extreme acts of penance—wrapping his chest in barbed wire, walking in shoes filled with rocks and broken glass that the conventional Mrs. Flood considers "trash"— are not normal, he replies that they are natural. He has come to learn that he must "pay," not for any specific sinful act as he had mistakenly thought as a child, but for his generally fallen nature. Finally, Haze rejects the home of and marriage to this conventional character. Similar to Harry Ashfield and Norton, who suffer abuse and neglect from their parents, Haze, being homeless, finds a home in the only way that can suit him as modern Manichean. As Wood has said of Ashfield, this young protagonist prefers drowning in the river, cradled in the arms of Christ, as it were, to the nihilism represented by his parents.[17] While Enoch, then, dons the ape suit and succumbs to bestiality in this modern bifurcated world, Haze, as hero, understands that "there's no other house nor no other city" (*CW* 129). There's no place else to be. To the modern audience, believers and unbelievers alike, this is tough medicine indeed.

As the history of critical commentary on this novel has indicated, the impact of O'Connor's religious belief on her first novel has led to a great deal of debate and confusion on the part of readers. Brinkmeyer has pointed out that the images of the desacralized world are unrelenting—so harsh and grotesque as to be unpalatable to the modern audience.[18] Her sacramental vision,

---

[17] Ralph C. Wood, "The Scandalous Baptism of Harry Ashfield: Flannery O'Connor's 'The River,'" *Inside the Church of Flannery O'Connor*, ed. by Joanne Halleran McMullen and John Parrish Peede (Macon GA: Mercer University Press, 2007) 201.

[18] Brinkmeyer sympathetically notes the harsh reaction of John Selby, O'Connor's editor at Rinehart, to the revisions that O'Connor had made to

as Asals has noted, almost doesn't seem evident in her portrait of this world and Haze's ultimate choice of death over life.[19] Feeley has argued that the seriousness of Haze's journey of discovery is undercut by the comic tone provided by Enoch;[20] and Sykes has recently noted, in terms echoing O'Connor herself, that perhaps this just isn't a fit age for Christian allegory.[21] O'Connor's own religious beliefs may indeed confuse readers, and her large body of writing on the subject has led to critics being primarily concerned with this religious dimension of her work. While this religious critical approach is invaluable for the insights that it offers, I believe that our understanding of the ethical interest that underlies her narrative vision can be enhanced by Gadamer's contemporary critique of modern scientism. What, in O'Connor's terms, is understood as our "fallenness" is made available in Gadamer's philosophical terms as our fundamental finiteness, our ontological and epistemological grounding within language and tradition, that prevents the autonomy of the reasoning mind over creation. His notions of the temporal nature of both knowledge

---

such original chapters as "The Train." *Wise Blood*, Brinkmeyer argues, marks the beginning of O'Connor's "mature fiction" and her movement away from "conventional satire and humor" toward a "harsh and strident narrator" (100–101) that will carry the fundamentalist vision of O'Connor's protagonists. As stated earlier, however, Brinkmeyer argues that the monologism of the narrative voice that endorses Haze's fundamentalist perspective is undercut ultimately by O'Connor's Catholic narrative voice (114–15).

[19] Frederick Asals, *Flannery O'Connor: The Imagination of Extremity* (Athens: University of Georgia Press, 1982) 56–57. Asals notes the "strong current of the imagery of repulsion, a repulsion at the physical deeper than anything required by the novel's motif of reverse evolution or the satire of a secularized society," and remarks the "empty and repugnant world of the novel" (50, 56).

[20] Feeley, *Voice of the Peacock,* 68–69.

[21] John D. Sykes Jr., *Flannery O'Connor, Walker Percy, and the Aesthetic of Revelation* (Columbia: University of Missouri Press, 2007) 50.

and art provide an instructive parallel to O'Connor's own incarnational notions of art and reality.

In his critique of the dualism of modernity, Gadamer, it will be remembered, follows Heidegger in his phenomenology of understanding as he defines it, not as an act of a reasoning subject holding sway over an object, but rather as an experience that resembles a dialogue between two partners. While Heidegger defines human understanding as a "thrown project" that necessarily involves prejudices that are clarified, put at risk, and altered during the process of understanding, Gadamer extends Heidegger's notion of the circular structure of understanding in his own description of understanding as "fusion of horizons."[22] Gadamer explains that this process of "fusion" always involves an element of "application." Due to our innate historicality, our cultural presuppositions, or the anticipation of meaning that we bring to our understanding of a text, Gadamer explains that a reader, or any interpreter of culture, never simply reads what is there. Rather, we are ourselves part of the meaning. We "belong" to the text in the same way that we belong to history. Because of our interest in what is said, we, therefore, "understand" a given text only when we apply its meaning to our own world. Thus, for Gadamer, understanding is always interpretation. The phenomenon of understanding consists of the creation of a new and comprehensive horizon that exceeds and includes the limited, historically specific horizon of each partner in the dialogue. The task of historical hermeneutics, then, as Gadamer explains, is not to cover up this tension between strange and familiar, past and present, but, respecting the radical temporality of human existence, to recognize it as the realization of the unified meaning that occurs in the mediated space where "I" and world meet (431). Time, then, for the historical hermeneutics of Heidegger and Gadamer is not a "gulf [that must be] bridged" in order to recover another's

---

[22] Hans-Georg Gadamer, *Truth and Method*, trans. Joel Weinsheimer and Donald G. Marshall (New York: Crossroad, 1991) 273.

meaning, but is the productive process in which all meaning, including that of the present, is rooted (264). Gadamer shares with Heidegger, then, the critique of pure perception upon which the objectivity of method is founded. For both thinkers, understanding is always interpretation, or re-creation, versus reproduction. Seen within the light of philosophical hermeneutics, then, the object of historical research is, unlike the object under the investigation of natural science, not an object at all. Our investigation is not governed progressively and teleologically by a desire to penetrate deeper and deeper into an object in order to attain a more "perfect" knowledge of it. Immersed as we are in history, it is not possible to gain a "perfect" knowledge of it. Rather, we must recognize that the historical object is the counterpart of ourselves, and that the event of understanding is a process by means of which we understand both history and ourselves in history (267).

Gadamer bases his analysis of the phenomenon of under-standing, generally, and his critique of method on a consideration of aesthetic experience, which, as experience, provides knowledge or understanding in the form of encounter or conversation. In doing so, he examines the meaning, or the achievement of understanding, particular to the experience of art in response to the subjectivist slant of modern epistemology. Gadamer conceives of the mode of being of the work of art, and of aesthetic experience, in terms of the metaphor of play. He explains that in play, the player loses him- or herself; the mode of being of play does not allow the player to behave toward the play as if it were an object (92). The player is not the subject of the game, but rather the play is, itself, the constant to-and-fro movement, which, directed toward no outside goal or purpose, continually renews itself. The play is, then, bound by the rules of the game and occurs in a closed-off playing field. The task of the player is simply the ordering and shaping of the continual movement of the game itself, and she fulfills her task successfully in simply representing it. As such, Gadamer describes the mode of being of play as self-representation. Gadamer distinguishes the mode of being of art from that of mere play, however, by explaining that in the performance of an artistic production, the "closed world ... lets down one of its walls," as it were. The play is no longer simply "represented," but is "represented for" someone. The being of art is, therefore, not exhausted by the fact that it represents, but it points beyond itself: the "closed structure includes the spectator" (98). As such, this "transformation into structure" suggests that the play has meaning—that it is intended to be understood (99). It is granted an ideality, and can, henceforth, be intended and understood as play. Thus, while it is dependent on representation, it can be separated from the particular representation and from its author; "it is a meaningful whole capable of repetition" (105). Such repetition, however—as Gadamer points out—does not mean that something is literally reproduced, or reduced to something original, but that every representation is "equally an original of the work" (110). Gadamer thus seeks to define the mode of being of the work of art in terms of temporality in order to understand the particular ontology of that which "comes to be in performance, and yet is still its own proper being that is represented there" (109). In doing so, Gadamer compares the being of the work of art to that of a festival which, he says, has as part of its being that it should be regularly celebrated. "Thus, it is its own original essence always to be something different" (110). Accordingly, the poetic work is given the intention of meaning through the ideality granted by structure, and yet is open to interpretation.

The temporality of the work of art thus points to its cognitive function. Just as Gadamer explains that the work of art is, in itself, a "meaningful whole," its meaningfulness is dependent upon performance, or interpretation. Thus, Gadamer explains that the structure of the play includes the spectator within its closed circle of meaning. At the same time, however, the spectator is set at an "aesthetic distance" that allows them a comprehensive sharing in what is being represented for them. Accordingly, as the spectator experiences an "ecstatic self-forgetfulness" in being "present," in opening themselves up to the possibility of being other, the distance also provides continuity with themselves. "It is the truth of [their] own world" that they recognize on stage and bring back to themselves (113). This encounter with "aesthetic being" is likewise, then, an encounter with the self.

Gadamer defines the truth encountered in the experience of art, then, as that of recognition. As such, he grants poetry the same cognitive value as did Aristotle when, in response to Plato's devaluation of the poetic work as a mere copy of a copy, thrice removed from the real, he describes poetic knowledge as knowledge of the essence—ironically that truth of being that Plato, through his dialectic, sought in the logos (103). In art, Gadamer explains, "what is" appears. Because the artist is pointing to something, he or she necessarily selects and distorts; the object of representation, then, appears as if refracted, illuminated, divorced from all chance and variable circumstance. It is grasped in its essence, or known "as" something. Therefore, though Gadamer can agree with Plato that an ontological gulf exists between the original and its artistic representation, he likewise asserts, with Aristotle, that the representation is "truer" than the material represented. That which appears in the work of art is that which we know, though heightened, elevated, and given meaning through structure. The mimetic theory of art is therefore granted cognitive significance as long as knowledge is considered to be knowledge of the essence—as is no longer the case, of course, in the nominalism of modern science (105).

Even a casual reading of the letters and essays of O'Connor will indicate the value and integrity that she attributes to the work of art. She responds to those who believe that her Catholic vision impedes her ability as a novelist by explaining that her Catholic vision is informed by her preoccupation with mystery, not simply by Catholic doctrine. Even to Catholic readers who expect to see only the pious represented in her work, she explains that they suffer from the same Manichean sensibility as her secular audience. "The basis of art," she explains, "is truth, both in matter and mode. The person who aims after art in his work aims after truth, in an *imaginative* sense, no more and no less" (*MM* 65[emphasis added]). In such unequivocal statements as these, she argues both for the autonomy of the work of art as well as its meaningfulness. In a discussion of Kafka's "Metamorphosis," she reminds us that although the fiction writer always begins with "what is or with what has the eminent possibility of truth about it," a "certain distortion" is used to reveal a deeper, or hidden, truth (97). (In the case of a story of a man who becomes a cockroach, she explains, the truth revealed is that of the dual nature of the human being.) Art, then, is revelatory and its revelation depends upon its independence from nature. O'Connor thus recalls Aristotle and anticipates Gadamer's reworking of Aristotelian theory as she explains that there "may never be anything new to say, but there is always a new way to say it," and in art the "way of saying a thing" becomes a part of the work of art itself. "You cannot say Cezanne painted apples and a tablecloth," she quotes John Peale Bishop as remarking, "and have said what Cezanne painted" (75). Art is not an abstraction, or the demonstration of a theme; rather the meaning of a novel is "embodied meaning." Appealing to the senses, the writer shows rather than tells her meaning. To read a story is to have an experience, she reminds us, and because it is an experience, it consists of an encounter that leaves us with "a renewed sense of mystery" (184).

This experience of mystery, central to O'Connor's notions of the sacramental nature of art, is apparent in "Good Country People"—the story of the undoing of Hulga Hopewell, arguably O'Connor's most notorious nihilist.[23] O'Connor held this story to be one of her best, and one she completed in an uncharac-

---

[23] Flannery O'Connor, "Good Country People," in *Collected Works of Flannery O'Connor*, ed. Sally Fitzgerald (New York: Library of America, 1988).

teristically short amount of time. The story involves the education of Hulga, the thirty-year-old PhD in philosophy. Here, as in her treatments of Asbury Fox of "The Enduring Chill," Julian of "Everything That Rises Must Converge," Calhoun of "The Partridge Festival," and Wesley of "Greenleaf," she juxtaposes her elitist intellectual against the attitudes of a provincial southern setting. In this case, Joy/Hulga has returned home after taking her degree, and, due to her heart condition, is destined to remain there, living with her mother. The contrast in attitudes is revealed from the outset as we are introduced to Mrs. Hopewell and her hired help, Mrs. Freeman. Mrs. Hopewell, as her name implies, always looks on the bright side of things and brings a naïve optimism to bear on the world's problems. Speaking in clichés, she tells Mrs. Freeman that "Nothing is perfect," "That's life!" and she expresses her belief that all people have their own opinions and that the world would be a better place if one would just smile. She values Mrs. Freeman and her two daughters, Glynese and Carramae, as "good country people," not "trash," and she isn't embarrassed to "take [Mrs. Freeman] anywhere" with her or "introduce her to anybody"(*CW* 264). She sees her own daughter, Joy/Hulga, who has taken a doctorate in philosophy, in contrast to the two Freeman girls who have already fulfilled the roles expected of them by social convention. Glynese is popular with boys, and Carramae, at fifteen, is already married and pregnant. She pities her own daughter, whose wooden leg (her leg having been shot off during a hunting accident) has prevented her from having any *normal* good times. Though Mrs. Hopewell is obviously satirized by O'Connor, she is also characterized as a caring, if critical, mother, a country-woman and an anti-intellectual who is bound by convention. A common O'Connor characterization, Mrs. Hopewell will act as foil to the protagonist, whose tale of education and seduction the story will tell.

The plot of the story involves the arrival at the Hopewell house of Manley Pointer, the country Bible salesman, whose encounter with the Hopewell women will forever change their lives. A nihilist parading as a "good country boy," he is able to dupe Mrs. Hopewell and Hulga, who see him only according to their own stereotypes. Mrs. Hopewell views him in terms of social status and values his professed decency, honesty, and work ethic, while the unbelieving Hulga, having had it with conventional Christians, pities this country Bible salesman as a simpleton whom she will be able to seduce and transform according to her philosophy. The story ends with Pointer turning the tables on Hulga, seducing her emotionally, though not sexually, stealing her wooden leg, and leaving her deserted in a barn loft.

Though the story of the nihilist Haze Motes may be open to charges of allegory, concrete dramatic details reveal a complex characterization of Hulga. Joy/Hulga was the victim of a hunting accident at the age of ten, and O'Connor doesn't spare details that reveal the trauma of the accident for the little girl. Her leg is literally "blasted off"; Joy never "lost consciousness" (267). A large blonde, with a wooden leg, who stomps around in a skirt and sweatshirt "with a cowboy and horse embossed on it," Hulga shows signs of never having left childhood. She also, because of the accident, has never been able to have a normal life, and has, therefore, been left, as her mother thought, emotionally vulnerable and stunted. A "brilliant" girl without a "grain of sense" (268), Joy/Hulga turns to the philosophy of "Nothingness" to allow herself, on her own terms, to transcend her very real limitations as a maimed child. She reads the writings of existentialist writer, Heidegger, who, in his critique of metaphysics, rebukes Science for its wish to "know nothing of Nothing" (269), and calls for a return to the acknowledgement of Nothingness.[24] In her own

---

[24] O'Connor herself would surely have "chilled," as she writes of Mrs. Hopewell, in such an encounter with the Nothingness asserted by Heidegger. It should be noted, however, that Heidegger's essay, "What is Metaphysics?" from which this quote is taken, offers a critique of the representational thinking of Western metaphysics that, in his view, will eventually lead to

desire for meaning and wholeness, she makes a religion of non-meaning that allows her to redefine herself in her own philosophic and humanistic terms. In religiously laden language, Joy renames herself Hulga, and rejoices in the fact that though her mother could not turn her "dust into Joy," her "greatest triumph" is that through this act of self-creation, she had been able herself to turn another's "Joy" into "Hulga" (267). As she perverts the Christian doctrine of Redemption that holds sway in this southern setting, she redeems herself through an act of the intellect. In answer to what she perceives to be the childlike imprecations of Pointer when he asks her to tell him that she loves him, she explains that she does "in a sense .... But it's not a word [she would] use." "I don't have illusions," she explains. "I'm one of those people who see *through* to nothing." She continues, revealing O'Connor's religious theme,

---

scientism. Heidegger's "Nothing" can be understood as the "no-thing." It is not an object that can be apprehended positively, once we have grasped the Platonic form or essence that lies behind it, therefore ordering it to abstract thought and making it available for use. Against the realm of ideational thought that has characterized Western philosophy and science, Heidegger asserts the temporality of knowledge and the disclosiveness of Being in which beings reveal themselves to us only to withdraw from us again. (I've noted O'Connor's affinity with some aspects of the existentialist tradition in an earlier footnote.) A good argument could also be made that Hulga indeed misunderstands Heidegger's meaning here. (I owe this insight to Ralph Wood.) She displays an attitude of scientism herself in her wish to dominate Pointer. She infantilizes him—she calls his kisses "sticky"—and assumes a will-to-power over him as she attempts to replace his purported Christian belief with her own belief in Nothing. Heidegger's own assertion of Nothingness, on the other hand, is an attempt to get back to the question of Being that science and philosophy have forgotten in their pursuit of beings as things or objects. Along these lines, it should be further noted that O'Connor shares Heidegger's appreciation for what he considers to be the disclosive power of language, particularly poetic language. In a letter to Beverly Brunson, dated September 1954, she recommends Heidegger's essays on Holderlin and references his notion that "the poet's business [is] to name what is holy" (*CW* 925). Such a notion is, of course, compatible with O'Connor's own understanding of the poet as "realist of distances."

"We are all damned ... but some of us have taken off our blindfolds and see that there's nothing to see. It's a kind of salvation" (280).

While Hulga seeks to educate Manley, however, it is he who educates her in a brutal demonstration of the ultimate outcome of this modern belief in Nothing. While O'Connor has used a sexual metaphor in describing Hulga's seduction, for Hulga—the PhD in philosophy—the seduction is a mental one. Her mind is described at their first kiss as "clear and detached" as it always is, and though the limited omniscient narrator tells the reader that Hulga was "pleased to discover that [the kiss] was an unexceptional experience and all a matter of the mind's control" (278), narrative irony tells the reader differently. Always intellectually in control, this girl responds physically, and returns Manley's kisses with increasing fervor. While Hulga believes that she will be asked to "prove" her love for Manley by sexually submitting to him, he wishes to only humiliate her. While she has made an idol of her wooden leg, replacing her injury, her vulnerability, and ultimately her unfulfilled sexuality, with this rational, wooden "crutch," Manley will steal the leg, revealing her deeper wound and the failure of her philosophy to heal this wound. In appropriately diabolical terms, Manley viciously undermines the identity Hulga has created for herself, as she—for once in her life—surrenders and lets down her guard. The impact of this surrender hits the reader hard as O'Connor uses religious language to show the limits of Hulga's rational reconstruction of herself.[25] When Hulga realizes that Pointer doesn't want a sexual encounter but would

---

[25] As Christina Bieber Lake has remarked in response to feminist critics who argue that O'Connor undermines the intellectual success of female characters, O'Connor's target here is not Hulga's impressive intellect but the choice she has made regarding what to do with the discovery of her humanity (*Incarnational Art*, 128). What O'Connor wants her to do with it, of course, is to give it to Christ, to join it with the suffering of Christ in order to show the possibility of Redemption, the transformation of suffering available through the Christian cross.

rather see where her leg joins on, she asks, "Why do you want to see it?" The boy gave her a long penetrating look. "Because," he said, "it's what make you different. You ain't like anybody else." "All right," she finally replies, and O'Connor notes: "it was like surrendering to him completely. It was like losing her own life and finding it again, miraculously, in his" (281). As Pointer disappears down the hole in the barn loft, with her leg "slanted forlornly across the inside of the suitcase with a Bible at either side of its opposite ends" and otherwise surrounded by his whiskey flask, his deck of cards with obscene pictures printed on them, and his contraceptives, Hulga is brought face-to-face with the real consequences of nihilism. Believing in Nothing, Pointer has annihilated Hulga by means of his own superior belief; he claims her leg—as symbol for her soul—as he asserts his own sovereign will over her.[26] O'Connor, of course, uses Pointer as a prophetic figure for Hulga. As she peers after him, O'Connor writes, she sees his "blue figure struggling successfully over the green speckled lake" (283). Here, the devil has indeed accomplished a great deal in order to lay the groundwork for grace to be effective. We don't know what will happen to Hulga next, but we do know that she and the reader have been shown the limits of her rational sovereignty.

In this story, then, O'Connor's protagonist is brought into a violent encounter that ultimately reveals to her the mystery of existence. Pointer is not what she thinks he is, her own vulnerability is revealed to her, and the limits of human nature are underscored for the reader. She has covered her injury with a wooden leg, touching the leg "with her eyes turned away," much like the shoe salesman—as a purveyor of artificial limbs—will do in the later story, "The Lame Shall Enter First," as he gingerly uncovers Rufus's deformed foot. While O'Connor notes that

---

[26] Ralph Wood has made a similar point regarding the fruit of nihilism as the assertion of Nietzschean will-to-power in studies of both the Misfit and Manley Pointer. See both "Good Country People" and "Strange Alliance."

Hulga had once felt shame regarding the wound that reveals her frailty, her "education had removed the last traces of that as a good surgeon scrapes for cancer" (281). The young girl, turned awkward crippled woman, will never dance, and it does not seem to bother the mature Hulga, who has replaced the needs of her flesh with the life of the intellect. O'Connor places Hulga's intellectualism into juxtaposition with the conventional views of her mother. As the drama of Hulga's transformation develops, Mrs. Hopewell's comic clichés are shown to be no more simple— and a good deal wiser, in fact—than the stereotypes that Hulga judges her by.[27] Only Mrs. Freeman seems to grasp the reality between these two poles. In referring to Joy as Hulga, she penetrates (almost Chillingworth style, it seems) "behind [Hulga's] face to reach some secret fact" about her and indicates with a look to Hulga that she shares "a secret" regarding the nature of her interaction with Manley that Mrs. Hopewell has not yet grasped (267). At the end of the story, Mrs. Freeman pulls her attention away from Pointer to the "evil-smelling onion shoot" that she is lifting from the ground. Seeming to recognize the mystery of human nature, she states: "Some can't be that simple ... I know I never could" (284). Obsessed throughout the story with hidden malformations and diseases, she functions for O'Connor as a voice that sees the bad and corrupted aspects of human nature, but is not interested in the good. Her own dualism thus suggests a puritanical perspective that will similarly be shown to be inadequate to O'Connor's own incarnational vision.

---

[27] Edmondson makes the apt observation that at least Mrs. Hopewell and Mrs. Freeman, as conventional characters, "accept the limitations of their mortality and can, in contrast to Hulga, live with a salutary everyday hope." At the time of her undoing by Pointer, Edmondson notes, Hulga, in contrast to her earlier condescension toward her mother and Mrs. Freeman, yearns for the "reliability inherent in those who can enjoy the predictability and safety of an ordinary life" (*Return to Good and Evil*, 80).

In "The Displaced Person" O'Connor develops the religious roots of Mrs. Freeman's cynicism through her portrayal of her two main characters, Mrs. Shortley and Mrs. McIntryre.[28] We first meet Mrs. Shortley as she ascends the hill of Mrs. McIntyre's farm, to look out for the arrival of the Guizac family. She appears as big as nature itself, a bulging granite mountain, who gazes at the surrounding countryside with eyes that appear as "two icy blue points of light that [pierce] forward, surveying everything" (285). She disregards the natural scene, ignoring the "white afternoon sun" and the peacock that follows her—O'Connor's two characteristic images of Christ and of divine order—as she waits for the intruder. Her characterization as a self-sufficient, self-righteous wife of a white farmhand is enhanced as she first glimpses the Displaced Person and his family. Her initial glance, O'Connor writes, grazes the tops of the heads of the Guizacs, slowly descending down on them as a vulture descends on a carcass. At this first meeting, Mrs. Shortley grudgingly admits to herself that they look like "other people," rather than the abstract images of the three bears that she had envisioned, "walking single file, with wooden shoes on like Dutchmen and sailor hats and bright coats with a lot of buttons" (286). She can't pronounce their name, and so calls them "Gobblehook," and instinctively snatches back her own hand when she sees Mr. Guizac, this man of foreign customs, bend to kiss the hand of Mrs. McIntyre, his new employer. As the story progresses, Mrs. Shortley's distrust of the Guizacs as foreigners is quickly shown to be based on her own Puritan/Protestant sensibility. A dualist, holding nature to be inherently corrupt, she fears that which she considers to be other, or extrinsic to herself, and as an adherent of an "advanced" religion, she credits reason ultimately with the ability to reform an imperfect reality. Thus, in her own comic terms, she first

---

[28] Flannery O'Connor, "The Displaced Person," in *Collected Works of Flannery O'Connor*, ed. Sally Fitzgerald (New York: Library of America, 1988).

compares the foreign son of Mr. Guizac unfavorably to her own son, H. C., who—equipped with eyeglasses that indicate clear vision—"was going to Bible school ... and when he finished ... was going to start him a church." "He had a strong sweet voice for hymns," Mrs. Shortley considers, " and could sell anything" (288). She reminds herself, when considering her own boy as a Bible student, that "none of the foolishness had been reformed out of [the foreigners' church]" (288). She considers the evil that she has seen on newsreels of this part of the world; she had seen "a small room piled high with bodies of dead naked people all in a heap, their arms and legs tangled together, a head thrust in here, a head there, a foot, a knee, a part that should have been covered sticking out, a hand raised clutching nothing." She reminds herself that "This was the kind of thing that was happening every day in Europe where they had not advanced as in this country." "Watching from her vantage point," O'Connor continues, "Mrs. Shortley had the intuition that the Gobblehooks, like rats with typhoid fleas, could have carried all those murderous ways over the water with them directly to this place" (287). She thus equates the Guizac family, and indeed the priest and the "Pope of Rome," with Europe, evil and mystery, with all that her reasoning mind cannot comprehend but that advancing civilization will one day be able to overcome. Her dualistic attitude is much the same as Hulga's. Just as the doctorate in philosophy "didn't like dogs or cats or birds or flowers or nature or nice young men" (268), so Mrs. Shortley's unseeing eyes, intent on her own "inner vision," dwell "directly in front of the peacock's tail," that "hung in front of her, [a map of the universe] full of fierce planets with eyes that were each ringed in green and set against a sun that was gold in one second's light and salmon-colored in the next" (290–91). Nature, corrupt from her Puritan/Protestant perspective, is intended to be transcended or reformed; a modern rationalist, Mrs. Shortley is not able to see its divine source. Her deracinated intellect that has banished God from creation allows her to see

143

people in hierarchical terms that pit those who are contaminated against those who are pure. She pictures "a war of words," in which the Polish words and the English words appear to stalk each other. She sees "the Polish words, dirty and all-knowing and unreformed, flinging mud on the clean English words until everything was equally dirty."[29] Similar to Rayber, the liberal reformer of O'Connor's second novel, Mrs. Shortley will, therefore, play the part of the avenging angel. Poring over her Bible, and believing she has a special part to play to fulfill God's plan "because she was strong," she has a prophecy (300). In a scene that the reader knows prefigures her fatal stroke, she proclaims, "The children of wicked nations will be butchered .... Legs where arms should be, foot to face, ear in the palm of hand. Who will remain whole? Who will remain whole? Who" (301). As a spokesperson and prophetess for enlightened values that can reform an imperfect reality—even if by methods of terror—she will restore the corrupt and chaotic world to fit her own image of order. Midway through the story, of course, it is she who is ultimately displaced. Leaving the farm to prevent Mr. Shortley from being fired, she suffers a final vision correspondent with the stroke that kills her. "All the vision in [her eyes] might have been turned around, looking inside her. She suddenly grabbed Mr.

---

[29] Lake provides a gloss on this important passage in O'Connor. In her discussion of Mrs. Shortley as a fundamentalist who must demonize "what she cannot understand," Lake interprets the words that Shortley envisions as "uncontrolled" since the words do not appear "abstract and controlled as *sentences*." The words, "distorted and disordering," are beyond Mrs. Shortley's rational grasp (*Incarnational Art*, 43). To my mind, O'Connor suggests here that the words *themselves* are, in fact, abstract and deracinated. They are cut loose from their place of meaningfulness within sentences, and are, therefore, frightening to Mrs. Shortley as they exceed her understanding. Perhaps the difference in Lake's and my own interpretation lies in her use of the word "abstract." In this passage of O'Connor, I take the sentences themselves to supply the physicality needed to make the words meaningful; the "words" are described by O'Connor as "just words, gabble, gabble, gabble, flung out high and shrill ..." (*CW* 300).

Shortley's elbow and Sara Mae's foot at the same time and began to tug and pull on them as if she were trying to fit the two extra limbs onto herself." Thus, the reader can infer from Mrs. Shortley's attempt to "rearrange the whole car" as she would have rearranged reality that this time her inner vision is one of judgment against herself: "her fierce expression faded into a look of astonishment," and her eyes close on the "tremendous frontiers of her true country" (304–05).

Unlike Mrs. Shortley, whose fear of the Guizacs is shown dramatically to have its roots in a Protestant dualism that results in a distrust of that which is other, that which she cannot understand and control, Mrs. McIntyre possesses an attitude toward the displaced family that is stated outright by O'Connor. Fighting to save her farm from the dissolution caused by the arrival of the Displaced Person, Mrs. McIntyre assumes a "set puritanical expression" against the priest who, operating from a basis of Christian charity, has reminded her that he knows she won't "turn [Guizac] out for a trifle" (317). For Mrs. McIntyre, however, who has run her farm for thirty years since the death of her first husband, the Judge, the unrest caused on her farm since the arrival of the Displaced Person is no mere "trifle." As she explains to the priest, Guizac is "extra …. He doesn't fit in" (316). She fears that his offer to Sulk of his young white European cousin in marriage will upset her Negroes, and she can't have them upset. As she explains to Guizac, "I cannot run this place without my niggers. I can run it without you but not without them" (314). The perspective that allows her to see people in such hierarchical terms as "trash," black laborers, and now this European "monster" who would violate class boundaries, will certainly not allow her to see them sacramentally as the priest does. Indeed, Mrs. McIntyre's face reddens at the mention, by the priest, of Christ, in the way that her mother's face had "reddened" at the mention of sex (317). Flesh, for the puritanical Mrs. McIntyre, has been devalued and is subsequently valued only in terms of its usefulness. Against all "sorry people" that have worked on her farm—the "Herrins and Ringfields and Shortleys"—Mr. Guizac she considers to be her "salvation," as she values his thrift, energy, and hard work that will help her run her farm. Her valuation of Guizac indicates that O'Connor has characterized Mrs. McIntyre, in terms of her proprietorship—a farm owner who sits in godlike judgment over the worth of her employees. As Mrs. McIntyre explains to Astor, whose knowledge of the Judge she feels has given him "a sense of title," "What you colored people don't realize ... is that I'm the one around here who holds all the strings together. If you don't work, I don't make any money and I can't pay you. You're all dependent on me but you each and every one act like the shoe is on the other foot" (308). In addition to her valuation of people in terms of their place on her farm, her proprietorial interests have gone a long way toward bankrupting her moral beliefs as she sees the suffering that Guizac has endured in Europe in terms of the opportunity it provides her. She tells Astor that she doesn't "have to put up with foolishness any more," for now she has somebody "who has to work." Indeed, though she knows that his life had consisted of struggle, Mrs. McIntyre's Protestant work ethic tells her "she knew what it was to struggle. People ought to have to struggle" (310). As a child, then, of the reformed church and enlightened values—as was her friend Mrs. Shortley—Mrs. McIntyre assumes a transcendent perspective that allows her to grant people their worth in terms of their utility, in terms that make *sense*. "Times are changing," she says to Astor, who acts throughout the story as a foil to her pretensions. "Do you know what's happening to this world? It's swelling up. It's getting so full of people that only the smart thrifty energetic ones are going to survive." "How come they so many extra," Astor asks. "People are selfish," she says. "They have too many children. There's no sense in it any more" (308).

In an important scene that foreshadows the killing of Guizac, O'Connor underscores the confidence of Mrs. McIntyre in her homestead and the values that sustain it. As Mrs. McIntyre climbs to the top of a slope and crosses her arms, she looks "grimly" out at the field of corn that Guizac is harvesting. 'They're all the same,' she muttered, 'whether they come from Poland or Tennessee…. "She narrowed her gaze until it closed entirely around the diminishing figure on the tractor as if she were watching him through a gunsight. All her life she had been fighting the world's overflow and now she had it in the form of a Pole. 'You're just like all the rest of them,' she said,'—only smart and thrifty and energetic but so am I. And this is my place…" (315). No wonder, then, that Mrs. McIntyre will tell the priest that Guizac is "extra" and that "he's upset the balance around here" (322). Similar to the Misfit whose words she echoes as a representative of the deracinated intellect, Mrs. McIntyre orders the world to fit her own scheme of meaning.

It is her dualistic worldview, then, that causes her to be complicit in the murder of the Displaced Person, and Mrs. McIntyre will lose her home—the one thing that she exclusively *does* value. After the death of Guizac, Mr. Shortley, who has come back to seek his rightful place on her farm, flees; Sulk heads to the southern part of the state, and it is implied that Astor, who "cannot work without company," also leaves (326). True to their characterizations, O'Connor enlists them ironically in the unraveling of her protagonist. As her reaction to the death of Guizac suggests, Mrs. McIntyre cannot live with what she has allowed herself to do. As she is "shocked by her experience," O'Connor writes that "Her mind was not taking hold of all that was happening. She felt she was in some foreign country where the people bent over the body were natives, and she watched like a stranger" (326). She has been displaced herself from that which she valued and allowed herself to believe; a "nervous affliction"—dramatized by such neurological symptoms as numbness in her limbs and a jiggling head—underscores the distance that lies between her old ways and current reality. At story's end, Mrs. McIntyre lies in bed, helpless, attended to only by a black woman and forced to listen to the priest who comes to visit and "explain the doctrines of the Church" (327).

Similar to Mrs. Shortley and Mrs. McIntyre, Ruby Turpin of "Revelation" will suffer a shock that will displace her from her visions of moral and metaphysical reality, but unlike her predecessors, Ruby will live to talk about it, or she will at least come to accept the vision that O'Connor grants.[30] Indeed Ruby Turpin, initially characterized as a large woman, self-satisfied, and jolly, emerges from her revelation physically unscathed and intent on "what lay ahead" (654). We are introduced to Ruby as she sits in the doctor's waiting room with Claud, waiting for him to be seen for his leg ulcer. She immediately takes the measure of those who wait with her. Noticing people's shoes, "without appearing to," Ruby notes her own "good black patent leather pumps" and the "red and grey suede shoes" that match the dress of the "well-dressed lady" and compares these to the tennis shoes and bedroom slippers of the white-trash patients (635). The scene in the waiting room consists of both spoken and inner dialogue in which Ruby expresses her gratitude and self-satisfaction at having been made by "Jesus" as she is. Complaining that she can't get her niggers to work unless she "butters them up," she discourses on the "way things are going to be" from now on (639). She thanks Jesus that she hadn't been made "a nigger or white trash or ugly" (642), but that she had been made just like herself and had been given a little of everything and the "wit to use it right" (654). She's not "white-trash," which "lounge[s] about the sidewalks all day" or sits around on the "Court House coping" and spits (639). Nor is she a nigger, as she explains to Jesus at the end, when she angrily confronts him over the violence done to her by Mary Grace, but she "could act like one. Lay in the middle of the road and stop traffic. Roll on the ground" (652–53). As a home-and-land owner,

---

[30] Flannery O'Connor, "Revelation," in *Collected Works of Flannery O'Connor*, ed. Sally Fitzgerald (New York: Library of America, 1988).

Ruby's values are similar to those of Mrs. McIntyre; her valuation of people in terms of their respectability and hard work is based ultimately in the dichotomous vision of her Protestant ethic that has banished grace from the world and, therefore, cannot value matter sacramentally. As a result, she keeps strict boundaries between herself and common folk, niggers, and white trash, but as a respectable land-owner, she works hard, goes to church, and gives help to the needy, whether "trash," white or black. In response to the white trash woman who wants all niggers sent back to Africa, she replaces inherent worth with pious cliché: "It's all kinds of them just like it's all kinds of us" (640).

What Ruby will learn, similar to Mrs. Shortley and Mrs. McIntyre, is that she, too, has a human nature that she holds in common with that which she considers most lowly or most ugly, and that the mystery of creation defies her rational understanding. Ruby's hogs act as a comic reminder to her and to the reader of her own common nature, just as they also ironically enforce her own notions of respectability. Her hogs are kept in a "pig parlor" where, elevated on concrete above the ground, they are hosed down every day and form part of her self-appraisal as the owner of a comfortable and efficiently run farm. To be called a "wart hog" from hell hurts Ruby more than does the book that Mary Grace hurls at her face. Confused and tearful at Mary Grace's action, Ruby asks herself why "she had been singled out for the message, though there was trash in the room to whom it might justly have been applied .... There was a woman there who was neglecting her own child but she had been overlooked. The message had been given to Ruby Turpin, a respectable, hard-working, church-going woman" (648). Later, in a similar rant that reveals her dawning religious awakening, she rails at God, "How am I a hog and me both? How am I saved and from hell too?" (652).

O'Connor's physical placement of her protagonist in the story's final scene works to undermine Ruby's self-satisfaction and conception of herself as she advances toward her revelation.

As Ruby asks, "How am I a hog?" "Exactly how am I like them?" O'Connor notes that she peers out over the pig parlor to the pasture and across to the cotton field and beyond to a "dark green dusty wood which they owned as well." As Ruby is the proprietor of the land, O'Connor writes that "She appeared to be the right size woman to command the arena before her," and indeed she has held sway over her acreage, the blacks who work for her, Claud, and now the hogs as she "jab[s] the stream of water at the shoats" (652). As has been foreshadowed at the beginning of the story, however, when O'Connor notes that at night, on the verge of sleep, Ruby's rigid class distinctions would break down until all the classes of people were "moiling and roiling around in her head" (632), here, too, O'Connor demonstrates the limits of Ruby's reason in trying to assign value and worth to people. "Go on," she yelled, "call me a hog! Call me a hog again. From hell. Call me a wart hog from hell. Put that bottom rail on top. There'll still be a top and bottom!" (653). What Ruby soon learns, though, is that just as the "pig astronaut" who—though an astronaut was still a pig—had died from being left unnaturally upright in his astronaut suit, she too will have to be content with her own nature, and no amount of respectability, hard work, and piety is going to get her out of it. As the "color of everything" that belongs to Ruby, "field and crimson sky, burned for a moment with a transparent intensity," Claud's "tiny truck" appears to her in the distance, carrying both him and their black workers. "At any moment," Ruby thinks, "a bigger truck might smash into it and scatter Claud's and the niggers' brains all over the road" (653). The suggestion here seems to be that Ruby is recognizing her own insignificance as a home-and-land owner. As she pairs Claud with her black workers and the devastation that may overtake them, she recognizes her own dependency on God and inclusion within a general mystery. Thus, as she gazes down into the pig parlor, Ruby appears to be looking "as if through the very heart of mystery," and she is granted "abysmal life-giving knowledge" in her revelation. Seeing a "vast swinging bridge extending upward from the earth," she notes all classes and types of people ascending it: she sees "white-trash, clean for the first time in their lives, and bands of black niggers in white robes, and battalions of freaks and lunatics." Finally, "bringing up the end," she recognizes those like herself and Claud, who "had always had a little of everything and the God-given wit to use it right." In the singing of hallelujahs, these stewards of "good order and common sense and respectable behavior … alone were on key," but she notes that even their "virtues were being burned away" (653–54). Stripped of her pretensions by the grace offered through the prophet Mary Grace, Ruby Turpin recognizes her own commonness, that her own nature is no different from that of white trash and black niggers.

Here, then, as in the stories of "Good Country People" and "The Displaced Person," O'Connor's protagonist undergoes a violent encounter that undermines the lens through which she views reality. As Kathleen Feeley has pointed out, both the religious and social realities of O'Connor's characters may be displaced.[31] The dualisms of her characters that represent a desacralized modern worldview assume different forms. Having severed itself from recognition of a common source, the deracinated intellect transcends matter and is able to mold reality to fit its own terms. Thus, Hulga, suffering greatly from the constrictions of the flesh in the youthful loss of her leg, constructs a woodenness around her soul that enables her to overcome the vulnerability that has been made all too clear to her in the loss of her full body function and her social life as a young woman. Believing in Nothing, she will not be disappointed again; not allowing her mother to turn her "dust into joy," she will "turn it herself into Hulga," as she redefines herself in terms that allow her intellectually to triumph over her ugliness and loss. Mrs. McIntyre, Mrs. Shortley, and Ruby Turpin perceive others in terms that

---

[31] Feeley, *Voice of the Peacock*, 22.

allow them to enforce the boundaries of their own social worlds. O'Connor gives McIntyre and Turpin, as landowners, command over their own domains, and they value people in terms of their usefulness to them, and according to the hierarchies determined by their notions of respectability. The hard work and propriety of these women will gain their salvation in rational terms. Against such confidence in the order achieved by Enlightenment rationalism, O'Connor brings the reality of mystery that inheres in her sacramental vision. Each character experiences the limits of her rational understanding, and is shown the reality of her dual human nature, that each is, as it were, a " hog and me both." For O'Connor as Catholic, however, the mystery of the Incarnation points to possibility as well as limitation. Matter is shown to be inherently good beyond our valuations of it as use; the concrete points beyond itself to the infinite. In a way that recalls Gadamer, then, in his assertion of the linguistic nature of existence and understanding, O'Connor will demonstrate the incarnational nature of both art and nature.[32] As Gadamer rethinks the truth

---

[32] In his analysis of the dualism that characterizes Western philosophy and science, Gadamer contrasts what he considers to be the linguistic nature of knowledge against a modern instrumentalist theory of language that assumes that language exists as a system of signs. Such an analysis points up the ethical consequences of modern dualism. Gadamer explains that since Plato's doctrine of ideas banished all knowledge to the intelligible sphere, "the proper being of words as such" first, within philosophical thought, lost any cognitive significance, or access to truth, that they held of their own (*Truth and Method*, 372). Plato's metaphysical model of original and copy by which he judged all phenomena suggested that words were merely one more appearance that had to be overcome in order to arrive, through pure thought, at the knowledge of true being. Thus words became signs or tools that were correct to the degree to which they represented the object or idea to which they pointed. Gadamer further explains that this "exclusion of what a language is beyond its aptitude as sign material" is at the heart of the scientific Enlightenment's ideal of a rationally constructed sign system of language in the eighteenth and twentieth centuries. To a system of unambiguously defined symbols would correspond the totality of the knowable—being itself—making it available for use (375). (Gadamer cites

claim of art against the modern methodological means of knowing, he asks us to consider what kind of experience of meaning it is in which nothing is objectively known, yet meaningful patterns of experience are revealed. [33] Similarly, O'Connor will demonstrate the reality of our finitude through the experience of art. Inherently incarnational, the work of art embodies mystery through its physical medium that enacts an encounter that leads us to self-knowledge. O'Connor thus reveals the ethical assumptions that lie behind her own incarnational notions of art and reality. O'Connor writes regarding the nature of fiction, "[It] is [the] product of our best limitations. Its dignity is an imitation of our own" (*MM* 192–93). Similarly, speaking to the experience of making art, but reflecting the reality of the efforts of our incarnate selves as well, she writes, "We can transcend our limitations best by staying within them" (171).

---

the usage of technical terms and the language of modern advertising as apt examples of the one-to-one correspondence that is inherent in a sign system of language. Such words, he explains, as terms, have been grasped from the life of language and have been "univocally defined" or granted one particular conceptual meaning [375].) Through this analysis of the progressive abstraction and devaluation of language, then—through which language becomes form, emptied of content, and at the disposal of a knowing subject—Gadamer can conclude that the knowledge of the modern natural sciences is "knowledge for domination" (375).

[33] Gadamer, *Truth and Method*, 431.

# 6

# THE HUBRIS OF THE SACRED SELF:
# MYSTERY, TRAGEDY, AND
# THE CHRISTIAN VISION

If the history of O'Connor criticism reveals anything, it is the impact of her stated religious beliefs on readers' understanding of her fiction. Critics such as Carter Martin, Kathleen Feeley, and John F. Desmond have offered major studies of the theological assumptions that underlie her narrative technique and symbolism, as well as the influence of her Christian religion on her fiction, generally. Ralph Wood has investigated O'Connor's interest in the consequences of nihilism in the modern world and has recently traced O'Connor religious concerns to issues in contemporary culture, as has Christina Bieber Lake. While this religious approach offers valuable insights, it can also issue in reductive analyses that look for point-for-point correspondences and that read—against all evidence, it would seem—O'Connor's Catholic belief as a doctrinal weapon that she wields against the world, and that enables her to conveniently escape involvement in social concerns by prioritizing the eternal and absolute.[1] Most critics

---

[1] See, for instance, Tim Caron. Caron seems to critique O'Connor for fiction that she doesn't purport to write. Drawing statements from her critical writings, he argues that her belief in Catholic doctrine holds in common with Southern evangelical Protestantism an emphasis on personal salvation rather than on issues of social justice. Throughout her letters and essays, O'Connor, however, argues that Catholic dogma and belief in such fundamental doctrines as sin, judgment, and redemption guarantees a respect for mystery. In her fiction, her characters are made to undergo an experience of mystery,

accept O'Connor's own assertions that Catholicism provides her with a respect for mystery, which inheres in matter, and that thereby creates a sacramental sense of creation. As she herself defines the Catholic novel, O'Connor states that it is not to be determined by subject matter, "but by what it assumes about human and divine reality" (*MM* 196). As I've argued in previous chapters, the American literary tradition of romance provides O'Connor with the flexibility needed to convey this sacramental sense, or her moral and artistic vision. What O'Connor's Catholicism and the genre of romance have in common is an interest in mystery and an insistence on the union of fact and fancy, or a conviction that eternal truths are apprehended through the world of the senses.

This belief that essential truths can be grasped only by returning to the world of things, objects, or phenomena is shared by developments in twentieth-century Continental philosophy. As Feeley points out, in August of 1955 in a letter to Betty Hester, O'Connor names Simone Weil and Edith Stein as the two women of the twentieth century who hold the most interest for her (*HB* 97–98). Feeley rightly explains that Edith Stein was a student of Edmund Husserl, the founder of modern phenomenology. While O'Connor's interest in Stein seems to dwell mainly in her conversion to Catholicism and, ultimately, in the suffering she encountered in her death at Auschwitz, the link between the philosophy of Stein and Husserl and Catholic sacramentalism

---

effected by grace, which undermines their rational self-understanding and brings them to an awareness of their own fallen nature. Such self-knowledge, for O'Connor, leads ultimately to charity, and to action. If the seasoned reader of O'Connor knows anything, it is that she doesn't expect much of us as fallible human beings. Caron, on the other hand, seems to expect too much. In his analysis of *Wise Blood* and the killing of Solace Layfield that helps to facilitate the conversion of the nihilist Hazel Motes, he laments the anagogical vision that "displaces the moral concerns regarding violence in the here and now" (*Struggles over the Word*, 47), and he seems to suggest that a didactic fiction could perhaps correct such worldly wrongs.

should not be overlooked. Turning away from philosophical idealism, as well as from the modern sway of logical positivism, Husserl attempted to close the age-old philosophical rift between subject and object by suggesting that our apprehension of reality actually consists in our encounter with objects, or in our experience or perception of them.[2]

Though we turn to things or objects in our daily life, Husserl argues that our experience is actually constituted by the meaning they take on for us. In his analysis of the phenomenological structure of our knowledge, Husserl explains that though as humans who, from our "'natural' standpoint" or perspective, tend to attribute primary reality to the objects we encounter, we are, nevertheless, aware of them also as signs or universals rather than merely as "fact."[3] As Erazim Kohak points out in his introduction to Husserl's thought, a necktie, for instance, is not simply an accessory to be worn around the neck, it means, in universally symbolic terms, "she loves me"; a new car suggests prestige rather than mere transportation.[4] Objects are thus important to us not for what they *are*, but for what they *mean*, and further through the objects themselves we can recognize common patterns that indicate the universal dimension of experience. By imposing an "eidetic epoche," that is, by "bracketing" or suspending the particulars of a given situation, we can apprehend the *eidos*, or

---

[2] Edmund Husserl, *Ideas: General Introduction to Pure Phenomenology*, trans. W.R. Boyce Gibson (New York: McMillan, 1931) 51–52. Husserl posits his new phenomenology against the empiricism of the natural sciences, which holds knowledge to be knowledge of discrete objects that exist as givens, independent of subjects, "out there" in the world. For a discussion of the developments of phenomenology and hermeneutics as they relate to theories of art and aesthetic experience, and to the ancient literary critical debate between Aristotle and Plato, see Howard Pearce, *Human Shadows*, 24–25.

[3] Ibid., 51–54. Husserl, *Ideas*.

[4] Erazim Kohak, *Idea and Experience: Edmund Husserl's Project of Phenomenology in* Ideas 1 (Chicago: University of Chicago Press, 1978) 7.

essence—the principle or generalities—that underlie it.[5] Such a process of "eidetic reduction" takes on added significance when we apply it to our social experience. Kohak provides an important gloss on the humanistic implications of the "eidetic epoche" when he points out that just as we "bracket" the instantiating facts that govern our knowledge of phenomena in order to discover the types and generalities that underlie reality, so also can we suspend the isolating particularities of our own immediate experience in order to grasp the universal principles and patterns common to all human experience. Thus, the significance of a snapshot of a Bushman with his arm around his wife and son is recognizable to those of us who live in Ohio (6), and, similarly, the grief of a friend whose son has died in an automobile accident is not alien to us, either, as the universal feeling of sorrow is common to us all, and our friend can always "fill us in on the details later" (98). We understand that, "because he is human," he is bound to feel a certain way (80), and it is the sense of human commonality, or shared experience, that allows us to extend our compassion. For Husserl's phenomenology, then, our understanding of objects includes a sense of an essence, or a recognizable pattern, through which the universal is suggested. He argues further that the importance of principles over factual instances and contingencies defines the incarnational nature of reality itself. "Sensory things are ... connected with physical things," he writes; there is no separation between physical reality and appearances or perception.[6] He suggests that the very nature of our physical bodies provides an apt example of the incarnational nature of essential reality: "Only through the empirical relation to the body does consciousness become real in a human ... sense," and capable of "mutual understanding" and communication about the world of which we are a part.[7] The tradition of phenomenology,

---

[5] Husserl, *Ideas*, 51–56.
[6] Ibid., 163.
[7] Ibid., 164–65.

then, shares with Catholicism, and indeed with O'Connor's choice of romance as narrative technique, a belief in the necessary union of the essential with the temporal, the universal with the particular. Ultimate reality must be grasped through the image or object. Dramatic action can make actual the mystery of human personality and existence.

O'Connor's own sense of the essential is revealed in what she describes as the anagogical vision of Catholic theology. Calling upon the method of medieval exegetes of sacred scripture, she explains the specific influence of such a vision on the reader or writer of a text as it allows that person "to see different levels of reality in one image or one situation" (*MM* 42). The fiction writer with anagogical vision, she explains, is "looking for one image that will connect, combine or embody two points; one is a point in the concrete, and the other is a point not visible to the naked eye, but believed in by him firmly, just as real to him, really, as the one that everybody sees" (42). Describing herself as a "realist of distances," O'Connor, it will be remembered, uses the expanded gaze of her sacramental vision to see "near things with their extensions of meaning" or to see "far things close up" (44). Her use of the grotesque thus provides a necessary distortion of the natural or ordinary intended to convey a sense of the larger mystery within which we live, that exceeds the finitude of our rational understanding, and to point out the ethical condition of a modern humanity severed from God's grace. Throughout her fiction, the anagogical nature of O'Connor's images is evident. Suns, moons, woods, and water all suggest a creation that mirrors its divine source—one that signals the presence of the Holy Ghost. Likewise, a wooden leg points to human limitation, to spiritual, as well as emotional sterility, and a clubfoot reveals the innate depravity of humankind, an essential aspect of our nature, or mystery, that cannot be explained away. For O'Connor's sacramental sense, the vulgar is always touched with the sublime. She quotes Baron von Hugel as stating that the Catholic anagogical vision recognizes that the "highest realities and deepest responses are experienced by us within, or in contact with, the lower and lowliest" (176). O'Connor's images, then, seek to reconcile spiritual distances, to evoke the presence of Christ or the presence of evil, and to disclose spiritual reality as well as possibility. Thus, an "artificial nigger" lawn ornament suggests the universality of pain and loneliness to her two initiates. A tattoo of a Byzantine Christ manifests the corporeality of God. The appellation of "wart hog from hell" leads toward revelation, and the Holy Ghost himself in "The Enduring Chill" descends from the ceiling of Asbury's room in the figure of an icy bird stain. Similarly, O'Connor's "agents of mercy" are very often "misfits," the likes of which include a satanic juvenile delinquent, a country Bible salesman, an acne-infested—"blue-faced"—anti-social teen, a hermaphrodite, and "some nigger's scrub bull" (*CW* 501).

This same Catholic, sacramental vision that informs her use of symbol likewise suggests an incarnational, and ultimately dramatic, theory of fiction. O'Connor explains that a "Catholic novel" is not properly to be defined by subject matter, as a reflection, for instance, of Christian or Catholic doctrinal truth, but as a fulfillment of her anagogical vision, representing reality as it is "manifested in this world of things and human relationships" (*MM* 172). Accordingly, everything, including the absolute, must be grounded in the concrete. Ideas must be given weight and extension (32), grace must be revealed through nature (153), and "mystery through manners," or through "the texture of life that surrounds you" (103). Only by fidelity to such concrete detail, to observed reality, O'Connor explains, can the writer hope to capture the sense of mystery he or she wishes to convey. The meaning of her fiction is finally, then, not abstract meaning, but experienced meaning, as it is embodied in the concrete literal action and imagery of the story. Throughout her criticism, she describes the influence of drama on her art. She explains, for instance, that "fiction is presented in such a way that the reader has the sense that it is unfolding around him .... Fiction has to be largely represented rather than reported. Another way to say it is that though fiction is a narrative art, it relies heavily on the element of drama" (73). As such, it is an "experience rather than an abstraction" in which "the characters are shown through the action and the action is controlled through the characters, and the result of this is meaning that derives from the whole presented experience" (90). For O'Connor, then, the story is a self-contained dramatic action through which is revealed "mystery as it is incarnated in human life" (176).

This concern for the dramatic enactment of mystery suggests an affinity between O'Connor's work and the spirit and technique of tragedy, as that genre which most profoundly embodies the reality of our dual human nature and hence conveys the fundamental experience of human limitation, common to O'Connor as a writer of romance-novels.[8] Indeed, throughout her critical writings, O'Connor discusses the formal aspects of her work in specifically Aristotelian terms. For O'Connor, as well as Aristotle, fiction must have a "beginning, a middle, and an end,"

---

[8] Other critics as well have pointed to this similarity between O'Connor's work and both the vision and form of tragedy. Howard Pearce, noting the correlation between such formal and thematic elements of tragedy as Aristotelian recognition and reversal and O'Connor's own Christian interest in such themes as "faith and rationality, pride and humility," argues for a reading of her fiction as tragicomedy, fusing both the Christian and tragic visions ("Ineffable Recognitions," 301). Marion Montgomery notes that O'Connor knows "the Greek dramatists more intimately than we sometimes recognize, and one cannot read her essays closely without becoming aware of her familiarity with Aristotle's *Poetics* or of her adaptations of Aristotle through the mediation of Saint Thomas" (*Why Flannery O'Connor Stayed Home,* vol. 1 of *The Prophetic Poet and the Spirit of the Age* [La Salle IL: Sugden, 1981] 45). Along these lines, he similarly observes that O'Connor's references to Aristotelian theory throughout her critical writing are evidence of her careful attention to craftsmanship and that this attention to detail, to the well-crafted work of art, mirrors the Thomistic influences on her art ("Realist of Distances").

though not necessarily in that order. "It must be selective, and what is there is essential and should create movement" (93). A writer's "moral sense must equal his dramatic sense" (*HB* 124), or, as Aristotle writes, actions and character reveal meaning and "moral purpose."[9] For both thinkers, the work of art is an autonomous structure held to the laws of craft rather than to a realistic representation of the external world.[10] (In her essay, "Catholic Novelists and Their Readers," O'Connor reminds us, in her characteristically wry language, of the need to adhere to the nature of things. The novelist, despite being a Christian, must be true to his nature as a writer, in order to avoid looking as foolish as the wolf that, after being converted by St. Francis, walked on his

---

[9] S.H. Butcher, *Aristotle's Theory of Poetry and Fine Art: With a Critical Text and Translation of* The Poetics, 4th ed. (New York: Dover, 1951) 29.

[10] In contrast to Plato, Aristotle explains that in art, the poet imitates the creative process of nature itself. He enhances the material represented in the interest of his own production and, therefore, creates an original. The standard of value for the work of art is therefore aesthetic law, as the aesthetic phenomenon is perceived to be a meaningful whole, independent of nature. As William Wimsatt and Cleanth Brooks point out in their classic New Critical study, *Literary Criticism: A Short History*, the difference in mimetic theory between Plato and Aristotle can best be explained in terms of their "views on universals" or ideas. Whereas Plato, as dualist, believes the form to be transcendent or separate from the appearance, Aristotle locates the form, or *eidos*, within the thing itself "as the dynamic principle of [its] being" (21–23). Such a conception would lead to an organic and formal theory of the work of art, in which the work of art would be fulfilled according to its own dramatic necessity. (O'Connor's affinity with the New Critics has already been amply noted by critics. See, for instance, John D. Sykes, Sarah Fodor, and Sarah Gordon. Gordon brings fresh insight to the study of the influence of the New Criticism on O'Connor by arguing that as a Southern woman writer, O'Connor aligns herself with the patrilineal traditions of both the New Critical school and the Catholic Church as a way of bringing power and authority to her own vocation as writer against the conventions of Southern womanhood [*Obedient Imagination* (Athens: University of Georgia Press, 2003)].)

hind legs.)[11] In a discussion that recalls the tragic flaw of the Greek hero, O'Connor writes that "drama usually bases itself on the bedrock of original sin, whether the writer thinks in theological terms or not" (*MM* 167). Quoting St. Cyril of Jerusalem, she further describes the subject of all good fiction as the mystery of human nature: "The dragon sits by the side of the road, watching those who pass. Beware lest he devour you. We go to the Father of Souls, but it is necessary to pass by the dragon" (35).

It is this "mysterious passage" past the dragon or "into his jaws" (35)—our struggle with our dual human nature—that most concerns O'Connor and likens her to the Greek tragedians. The grandmother in "A Good Man Is Hard to Find," like the Greek hero, stands on the brink of death, recognizing her culpability, and possibility, in the face of the eternal. As such, O'Connor explains that while a "great tragic naturalism" may provide a moving representation of the forces that condition our lives and, therefore, determine our actions, she is interested in the free and open action, the response of characters who, in a mysterious universe, are forced out beyond the ordinary "to meet evil and grace," and "who act on a trust beyond themselves," whether they recognize the source of this trust or not. O'Connor explains that the serious fiction writer, like the tragedian, is interested in "possibility rather than in probability," "in what we don't understand rather than in what we do," and therefore in action that makes contact with

---

[11] Flannery O'Connor, "Catholic Novelists and Their Readers," in *Mystery and Manners: Occasional Prose*, ed. Sally and Robert Fitzgerald (New York: Farrar, Straus and Giroux, 1969). Similarly, Aristotle employs an example from the animal kingdom when he observes the difference between accidental errors in poetry, and those that touch its essence. If the poet portrays a horse with both its right legs thrown forward at once, for instance, Aristotle explains that while the poet does not here provide a mirror image of reality, the inaccuracy is not detrimental to the integrity of the poem itself.

mystery (41–42).[12] In describing her use of the grotesque as a distortion of the ordinary, bent toward the revelation of mystery, O'Connor explains that though the writer expresses "mystery through manners," "grace through nature," there must always "be left over that sense of Mystery which cannot be accounted for by any human formula" (153). It is, likewise, into such an experience of mystery, or "wonder," at the ironic turn of events and, therefore, at the incomprehensibility that surrounds human existence, that tragedy wishes to move us.

To accomplish this, the tragedians rely upon the element of "surprise" as described by Aristotle in his *Poetics*. Aristotle explains that the success of tragedy depends upon the tightly constructed unity of all its parts. Plot, character, thought, diction, song, and spectacle all work together to form a complete dramatic action, the end of which is the "proper purgation" of the emotions of pity and fear.[13] Most crucial to the success of the tragedy is the

---

[12] One recognizes immediately here the similarity between tragedy and romance as defined by Hawthorne and adopted by O'Connor. The romance genre gives the writer latitude from the "probable" or everyday as he or she portrays reality "under circumstances ... of [his or her] own choosing or creation" (Hawthorne, Preface vii). This very latitude claimed by the poem is articulated by Aristotle when he explains that tragedy differs from history in terms of its portrayal of universals. While history must concern itself with facts, with what *has* happened, tragedy concerns itself with what *would* happen in accordance with probability or necessity. In a radically different idiom and time, O'Connor echoes this universal dimension of the work of art when she writes in her essay, "Writing Short Stories," that a local southern neighbor of hers points out in response to reading some of her short stories that "them stories just gone and shown you how some folks would do." O'Connor reflects that "that was right; when you write stories, you have to be content to start exactly there—showing how some specific folks *will* do, *will* do in spite of everything" (*MM* 90). For further discussion of the universal dimension of romance and Aristotle's *Poetics*, see Richard Chase and his comments on William Gilmore Simms's definition of romance as articulated in his Preface to *The Yemassee* (15).

[13] Butcher, *Aristotle's Theory of Poetry and Fine Art*, 23.

element of plot, or the "orderly arrangement of [its] parts."[14] Additionally, the structure of the whole must be organic; all action must form one action and be joined by "the law of probability or necessity ...."[15] Stemming from this governing law of reason, or "probability," and equally important to it, is the element of "surprise," which in combination with "probability," produces the sense of "wonder." As Aristotle explains, the element of "surprise" must grow naturally from the plot, following as "cause and effect," but at the same time, must be a coincidence. The effect of tragic wonder will be greater if the coincidence has an "air of design."[16] The two elements of "probability" and "surprise" are interdependent; it is upon their synthesis that the emotional import of *peripeteia* and *anagnorisis* (reversal and recognition) depends and the moral and metaphysical weight of the tragedy, the sense of "wonder," is based.

In similar fashion, O'Connor attributes the success of her stories to what she calls a "reasonable use of the unreasonable." Such an element in her fiction, she explains, signals where the "real heart of the story lies" and is manifest in the "significant gesture" (*MM* 111). She explains that in each story there is a moment, an action or gesture by an individual, which indicates that grace has been offered. Through this action of grace the character may transcend any expectations the reader has of her, any "neat allegory" or "pat moral categories" that have been assigned her. Such a gesture, O'Connor explains, exists on the anagogical level. It is "both in character and beyond character" suggesting "both the world and eternity" (118). Toward this end, toward, for instance, the grandmother reaching out to the Misfit, O'Connor bends the entire story, all language, imagery, and action (162). There is a careful piling up of detail, and her images accumulate anagogical meaning to indicate the final anagogical

---

[14] Ibid., 31.
[15] Ibid., 33.
[16] Ibid., 39.

action of the story. The Misfit, for instance, appears on the first page of "A Good Man Is Hard to Find"; the exposed beams in the attic cast foreboding shadows long before Norton hangs himself in "The Lame Shall Enter First"; and in *The Violent Bear It Away*, the continual presence of water, early on in the novel, signals Bishop's fatal baptism. The gesture, then, when it happens, is "both totally right and totally unexpected." It makes contact with mystery. It marks, for O'Connor, the moment of grace, and it carries enough "awe" (11), enough shock value, to jar the reader into an emotional recognition of its significance.

Such a gesture determines the nature of the hero in tragedy. As Richard Sewall explains in *The Vision of Tragedy*, the meaning of tragedy lies not in the intervention of fate or destiny in an individual's life, but in the action or "gesture" that the individual, acting free and "unaccommodated," offers in response.[17] The gesture, then, tests the worth of the hero; it determines his or her capacities in the tragic situation. Such a gesture, or action, is offered in the "boundary-situation" presented by the tragic dilemma, a situation, Sewall writes, of "extreme pressure," in which the individual, pushed to the "limits of his [or her] sovereignty," acts in response to the insoluble conflict presented him or her by the tragic circumstances (5). As such, this response constitutes the "discovery" of the tragedy; it points to whatever truth or human meaning can be gleaned from the drama, as an experience of human nature (16). It is prophetic in that it transcends the world of which it is a part, the established values of society, offering new insight into the human situation and an answer to the existential question of "how to live."

In O'Connor's fiction, of course, such a gesture issues from the violent situation. As O'Connor explains, "violence is never an end in itself. It is the extreme situation that best reveals what we are essentially" (*MM* 113). It "reveals those qualities least

---

[17] Richard Sewall, *The Vision of Tragedy* (New Haven CT: Yale University Press, 1980) 16.

dispensable" in our personalities that are all we have left to take into eternity with us, to offer to God as the cost of our salvation (114). After the death of her entire family, and immediately before her own death, the grandmother reaches out to the Misfit as she transcends her superficial understanding of the deep mystery she "[had] been merely prattling about" (112). Recognizing the Misfit's torment and her own place of responsibility within the human family, she offers him the touch of consolation. Such a gesture marks the moment at which grace is accepted or rejected. It secures the grandmother's salvation and conveys O'Connor's vision of Christian charity, her concern for compassion and empathy, to the reader.

This gesture, therefore, points to the ethical implications in O'Connor's fiction. In her discussion of the distinction between Aristotelian and Platonic mimetic theory as it pertains to the genre of tragedy, philosopher and literary critic Martha Nussbaum points to Aristotle's conception of an "ethical universe" as the source of his appreciation of the values and insights offered by tragedy. Unlike Plato, she explains, who believes that as human beings, in order to lead a good or ethical life, we must overcome the irrational elements of ourselves, our emotions, for instance, and sexual passions, Aristotle believes that as social beings, our ethical life is dependent upon external events, or the world, as it impinges upon us. He, therefore, advocates a form of "practical rationality" that will allow us to be "self-sufficient in an appropriately human way."[18] By presenting the role of contingency, luck—or what the Greeks called *tuche*—in our lives, tragedy demonstrates the inability to eliminate conflict from our lives and allows us to learn about our own values and ethical choices by noting our emotional responses to the choices made by the hero, torn by the conflicting claims of the tragic dilemma (3). Because it acknowledges the

---

[18] Martha C. Nussbaum, *The Fragility of Goodness: Luck and Ethics in Greek Tragedy and Philosophy* (New York: Cambridge University Press, 1986) 8.

claims of *eros*, Nussbaum explains, the values disclosed by tragedy are social or "other-related" and are, therefore, suggestive of wonder as the appropriate response to the mystery inherent in the tragic experience (20). Within this context, she examines the ethical choices made by heroes who are tested by their passional, as well as intellectual, responses to the conflict situation. She argues, for instance, that while Agamemnon did the right thing in sacrificing the life of his daughter, he was guilty of feeling the "wrong way." Convinced that he had "reasoned well," that he had resolved the conflict, he was able to kill his daughter without regret. He moves, then, "from horror to confidence and complacency" (35), unable to feel the force of the tragic dilemma confronting him. In *Antigone* as well, Nussbaum points out the implicit criticism of this desire to control and simplify the world, to eliminate the claims presented by the tragic conflict. Creon, for instance, "guilty of too much faith in human progress and the controlling powers of reason and order" (77), omits all claims upon the individual except that of civic duty. With the death of his son, he learns a painful lesson regarding the claims of his own humanity. Finally, Antigone herself denies the claims of "eros," as she refuses to temper the claim of her pious obligation to bury her brother with the claim of love asserted by her living sister. Tragedy, then, as Nussbaum explains it, presents us with a criticism of the human desire for rational self-sufficiency or the desire to control or eliminate conflict through the power of reason.

Within her Christian context, O'Connor defines the limitations of human reason specifically in terms of modern humanity, marked, since the Enlightenment, by a decreasing dependence upon God and an increasing faith in the powers of the human intellect and, subsequently, in the ideal of progress. For O'Connor, modern humanity is characterized by an increased rationalism and subjectivism. She explains that our vision stops at the sides of our own skulls (*MM* 200); the "reaches of [our] reality end very close to the surface" (157). Turning from God, we have turned into ourselves. O'Connor believes that we are no longer interested in going outside ourselves, but rather are concerned with the impingement of the world, a "meaningless absurd world," on the sacred self (158).

The pages of O'Connor's fiction are filled with the conesquences of such modern subjectivism and enlightened rationalism and with the failed projects of liberal reformers that often end tragically for themselves and others as they are motivated neither by love nor compassion but by the demands of the ego of the reformer.[19] Hulga, for instance, the nihilist PhD in "Good Country People," believes in "Nothing" and understands everything *but* the mystery of evil. Attempting to dupe the ostensibly naïve country Bible salesman, she ends up a victim of his own superior nihilism, left without a leg in a deserted loft. Julian in "Everything That Rises Must Converge," similarly convinced of his own moral and intellectual superiority to the Southern provincialism that surrounds him, isolates himself within a "mental bubble" from which he observes, and passes judgment on, the "general idiocy" of his fellows (*CW* 491). Priding himself on his own liberalism, he attempts to teach his foolish but innocent mother a lesson in racism and in the process humiliates her and precipitates her fatal stroke. In "The Lame Shall Enter First," Sheppard, another of O'Connor's liberal reformers, is offended by the juvenile delinquent Rufus's taunting him about Christ and salvation, and, ignoring Rufus's own professions of evil, attempts to "save" him himself, relying on the sociological insights he has gained as "City Recreational Director" and weekend reformatory counselor. He neglects the physical and emotional needs of his own young son, who has just lost his mother, because he is intent on saving Rufus, who has a higher IQ than Norton. He finally realizes his own moral poverty, of course, when Norton commits suicide in the hopes of joining his dead mother in eternity. In a similar case,

---

[19] The fates of O'Connor's liberal reformers recall, of course, Hawthorne's Aylmer, Giovanni, and Hollingsworth.

Rayber, a psychology teacher in *The Violent Bear It Away*, attempts to educate his nephew Tarwater away from his calling as a prophet. He neglects his own retarded son Bishop, whom he considers a mistake from God, and, not heeding the signs of Tarwater's desperate spiritual struggle about baptizing Bishop, allows Bishop to be drowned—though baptized—by Tarwater. Finally, most horribly characteristic of the modern subjective sensibility are the empiricism and nihilism of the Misfit in "A Good Man Is Hard to Find." He cannot believe in Jesus because he "wasn't there" to witness the death and resurrection; consequently, in his desire to find meaning that will sustain his life, he believes that Jesus has "thown everything off balance" for him (*CW* 151). Believing in only what he sees with his own eyes, he sees nothing, and can believe in nothing. Life makes no sense for him, and as an intelligent nihilist, he constitutes his own life meaning through acts of destruction.

Egoism, then, or spiritual and intellectual pride, constitutes the root conflict in O'Connor's fiction, and the growth of her characters involves a humbling of that pride. Through the violent situation, those characters who would aspire to rational self-sufficiency are brought to a recognition of the "humility" that O'Connor, as Christian, believes comes with "self-knowledge," or with the knowledge of nature that is severed from God's grace (*MM* 35).

The reader's own response to O'Connor's fiction, the experience of mystery that she hopes to render, turns on irony. Aristotle explains that the experience of tragic "wonder" depends upon an ironic turn of events, the reversal of fortune, the import of which ultimately rests on identification with the tragic hero. "[P]ity is aroused by unmerited misfortune," he explains, "fear by the misfortune of a man like ourselves."[20] Similarly, if we are to grant O'Connor's characters the "special kind of triumph" that she

---

[20] Butcher, *Aristotle's Theory of Poetry and Fine Art*, 45.

calls for, then they, as she herself suggests, cannot be "altogether bad" (*MM* 111); we must be able to see something of ourselves in them. The grandmother, for all her duplicity and conventionalism, resembles our own "grandmothers or great-aunts" (110). Julian, despite his cold-hearted and simple-minded condescension, is pathetic as he enters the "world of guilt and sorrow" at the story's end (*CW 500*). O'Connor's characters are neither wholly good nor bad, as she herself suggests, and though they carry a "burden of meaning larger than [themselves]," they share as well in a "specific human situation" (*MM* 109). Like the Greek hero, then, O'Connor's characters—even her grotesques as they serve a prophetic function—point to ordinary humanity, just as the role of contingency in life, dramatized by the reversal of fortune, suggests what can happen in human life, generally. Such identification is therefore central to the ethical import of tragedy.[21] The insights gained by the hero, through their experience of suffering, render knowledge into our own human situation and are intended to disclose insight into our own values as we attend to our emotional responses to their suffering. [22] As Gadamer reminds us in his

---

[21] As discussed earlier, the identification with the hero of tragedy is a crucial distinction between Aristotelian and Platonic mimetic theory. Aristotle's inclusion of the spectator within his definition of tragedy enables an understanding of the nature of knowledge gained through our experience of art. Unlike Plato who considers the work of art to be a static reflection of an unchanging, ideal reality, Aristotle views tragedy as an imitation of humans' *actions*. Similar to O'Connor's conceptions of the nature of short fiction, then, there is the possibility for growth, change, and conversion. Characters are, therefore, not simply good or bad, static figures whom we must reject or admire, but are, like O'Connor's grandmother, very much like ourselves, human beings with whom we relate, and at whose suffering we experience a certain pity and fear.

[22] Nussbaum recalls Gadamer's discussion of the value of the tragic emotions in her own understanding of the cognition gained through our experience of tragedy. She traces the etymology of the word *katharsis* to suggest a meaning of clarification—the removal of obstacles, for instance, to correct perception—rather than simply purgation (389). As such, the

analysis of the cognitive value of tragedy, it is through our identification with the suffering of the hero that we recognize our own experience, and our own finitude in the face of mystery. Oedipus demonstrates his newfound knowledge of the reality of his own limitation as he stabs out his eyes to indicate his former blindness; Hazel Motes, at the end of O'Connor's novel, puts out his eyes *in order to see*: "if there's no bottom in your eyes, they hold more" (*CW* 126). What Hazel now *sees* is the depthless mystery that surrounds him.

O'Connor's Catholic vision provides her with a sacramental sense of creation that asserts that grace inheres in matter or that the "image of ultimate reality" can be "glimpsed in some aspect of the human situation" (*MM* 158). Though indeed Catholic, such an anagogical vision shares with Husserl's phenomenology a belief in the essence, or universal, that lies within the object. Through our experience of sensible reality, we can apprehend patterns that point to our commonality, that suggest our likeness, beyond the particulars of difference. This same sense of the universal, and of the timeless that is revealed through the temporal, is shared by Aristotle as well as he articulates the vision that is embodied in the formal structure of tragic drama. As is clear from her many statements on the concrete, sensuous nature of fiction, O'Connor's incarnational vision of reality ultimately informs a dramatic theory of fiction. As the sacraments of her theology point to the Christian mystery that exceeds rational understanding, her intention to dramatize the mystery that surrounds our existence likens her to writers of tragedy. O'Connor's own purpose in dramatizing mystery is to call into question the confidence of Enlightenment rationalism as it underlies both modern subjectivism and the ill-conceived projects of her secular reformers. As she renders an experience of mystery to both character and reader, she points up

---

cathartic effect produced by the tragic emotions of pity and fear contributes to our self-understanding rather than performing the simple task of ridding ourselves of unhealthy emotions.

the finitude of human existence, the incompleteness, or "original sin," that tragic drama throughout the ages has shown to be an essential aspect of the human situation. To the extent that we can identify with her characters or recognize in O'Connor's grotesques ordinary suffering humanity, we can experience with them the ethical yield of this encounter with mystery. We can recognize our own commonness and the subsequent need for charity or compassion, or we can—at the very least—feel the horror suffered in a world without grace while watching as an entire family, albeit a grotesque one, is murdered by the modern nihilist.

# CONCLUSION

In her "*Introduction* to A Memoir of Mary Ann," Flannery O'Connor relates an experience that demonstrates, in concrete terms, the beliefs behind her attraction to the life and works of Nathaniel Hawthorne. In this essay, O'Connor tells of a letter she receives from Sister Evangelist, the Sister Superior of Our Lady of Perpetual Help Free Cancer Home in Atlanta, requesting that O'Connor write an account of Mary Ann, a patient who lived under the care of the sisters until she died at age twelve. The sisters wanted a writer who would be capable of capturing the little girl's bravery, charm, and spirit in the face of her illness. O'Connor, with her characteristic distaste for the sentimental and her strongly held notions of the proper vocation of her art, declines and re-assigns the task of writing to the sisters themselves, believing that it could be better accomplished by those who knew her. Before returning the picture of Mary Ann that the sisters had enclosed, however, O'Connor reflects on the photograph, noticing the malformation of one side of the face caused by the cancerous tumor, but noticing as well, the beauty and brightness of the other side. Such reflection, O'Connor writes, leads her to her bookshelf, to Hawthorne's story, "The Birth-mark," and to that "wonderful section of dialogue where Aylmer first mentions his wife's defect to her." At the conclusion of this opening dialogue, Aylmer suggests to Georgiana that the defect on such a face as lovely as hers shocks him "as being the visible mark of earthly imperfection." O'Connor's reflections end on Georgiana's response; the young bride, deeply hurt, cries out, "You cannot love what shocks you!" (*MM* 216). Here, Georgiana rightly understands the limits that her birthmark imposes on her husband's ability to love her. The photograph of Mary Ann's face, twisted and misshapen, as well as this account of the interaction of Georgiana and Aylmer, leads O'Connor to reflect on the nature of the grotesque and the sacramental.

As a Catholic, O'Connor believes that grace inheres in matter and, therefore, though the material world may be flawed, it is essentially good, as it was created by God. Aylmer, unwilling to rest with an imperfect creation, wishes to transcend matter in order to aspire to pure spirit, to an image of ideal reality. Seen within O'Connor's Catholic context, then, he, like her own character Rayber, is infected with the ancient heresy of Manicheism. Having banished grace from nature, the secular deracinated mind reduces mystery to problem, and brings all of material being within the domain of human subjectivity. The acts of kindness of O'Connor's liberal reformers are, therefore, empty and often disastrous—as the deaths of Georgiana and also of O'Connor's Norton and Bishop make clear—because they are based in acts of abstraction instead of compassion, and are motivated by the ego of the reformer.

O'Connor shares not only her vision of human limitation but also the literary mode needed to convey this vision, with Hawthorne as her literary precursor. As Hawthorne defines the romance as genre, he explains that it is not held to a naturalistic or realistic representation of reality, but instead presents reality as it is conceived in the mind. The creative mind of the romance writer conceives a "neutral territory," blurring the distinction between inner and outer reality. The romance thus allows O'Connor the freedom to convey her sacramental vision, to distort reality in order to reveal a hidden reality; as it combines judgment with vision, it allows for the re-association of sensibilities that the modern bifurcated mind has sundered. It, therefore, allows her to convey her vision "whole" to the modern audience that, as she suggests, may expect either the "pious" or the "pornographic." For O'Connor and Hawthorne, then, the form and substance of romance provide the means by which they are able to convey their critique of the dualism of modernity. As it blends fact and fancy, romance calls into question the dichotomy between subject and object upon which modern scientific objectivity is founded, and it points toward the reality of mystery, toward that which cannot be rationally apprehended. Hawthorne's characters—his artists, scientists, and religious and philosophical idealists—are thus all liable to commit the Unpardonable Sin as they attempt to penetrate the secrets of the human heart in an effort to know and ultimately control the nature or actions of another. O'Connor, as Catholic, conveys the mystery of existence according to the sacraments of her theology. The material world is co-extensive with the eternal and absolute; the heroes and heroines of her romance-novels and short stories are called out from the ordinary or everyday into a confrontation with grace that yields an experience of mystery. As they are shown the limits of their rational understanding, they, like Hawthorne's characters, are brought to recognition of their finite nature.

This notion of mystery, of the temporality of existence, and of the truthfulness that is conveyed by art, is shared by the hermeneutics of Gadamer, whose critique of Enlightenment rationalism can enhance our understanding of the ethical visions of O'Connor and Hawthorne. Against the subjectivism of modernity, Gadamer argues that the achievement of understanding occurs in a "fusion of horizons" that includes and exceeds the limited perception or horizon of each partner to the dialogue. He bases his understanding of the dialogic nature of knowledge on his speculations concerning the experience of art. Resisting Plato's conception of the work of art as a mere copy, or a sign pointing toward an eternal, timeless form, Gadamer follows Aristotle in asserting that aesthetic experience provides a truth of its own. Gadamer thus posits a mimetic theory of art against the dualism of Plato's correspondence theory. In this understanding, the artist does not simply replicate a timeless truth, but rather she imitates the creative process itself, as she constructs a formal object, freed from external criteria and held to the laws of its own nature. As such, the work of art is granted autonomy, and our experience of it is one of encounter that yields new knowledge about self and the world that the work represents. The work of art is thus seen to have a transformative or reflective value. By a process of selection, Gadamer writes, the artist heightens and gives new meaning to the raw material of existence, so that which is revealed is shown *as* something. The cognition brought about by art, then, is one of recognition; the reader or spectator recognizes an essence, or a universal, that underlies human experience.

This concern for the universal and essential, rather than the nominal and the subjective, has to bring us back, then, to the work of O'Connor and Hawthorne. As O'Connor reminds us, in her "*Introduction* to A Memoir of Mary Ann," the imperfection of Mary Ann's face reveals that the "good" in all of us is something "under construction"; like the seventh day of creation, it remains for us to finish. As she rejects the pervading sentimentalism of modernity in this essay, O'Connor notes that Bishop Hyland, preaching the funeral service of Mary Ann, cannot imagine the world beyond her family and friends, who would not wonder why she had to die, but rather would question "why she should be born in the first place" (*MM* 226). Against the Enlightenment rationalism that has resulted in the bifurcation of the material and the devaluation of matter, O'Connor asserts her sacramental vision and the sacramental nature of art. The experience of art yields new knowledge and reveals our finitude and temporality. As it engages us in an encounter, it shows the achievement of self-knowledge to be an ongoing process and demonstrates something essential and universal about our nature. O'Connor remarks that Hawthorne recognizes this universal when, under the guise of the "fastidious gentleman" whose action he describes in *Our Old Home*, he stoops to pick up the young foundling in the Liverpool workhouse. Similarly, Rose Hawthorne, Hawthorne's granddaughter, recognizes our universal nature when she founds the Catholic Order whose sisters will eventually care for Mary Ann. For the writer of romance, then, the work of art points to the possible, not merely to the probable. Working through the actual and the concrete, it demonstrates the reality of our common nature. Given the depth of what it has to reveal, Hawthorne would surely have agreed with O'Connor that "it requires considerable courage at any time, in any country, not to turn away from the storyteller" (35).

# BIBLIOGRAPHY

Allen, William Rodney. "The Cage of Matter: The World as Zoo in Flannery O'Connor's *Wise Blood*." *American Literature* 58 (1986): 256–70.

———. "Mr. Head and Hawthorne: Allusion and Conversion in Flannery O'Connor's 'The Artificial Nigger.'" *Studies in Short Fiction* 21 (1984): 17–23.

Asals, Frederick. *Flannery O'Connor: The Imagination of Extremity.* Athens: University of Georgia Press, 1982.

———. "Hawthorne, Mary Ann, and 'The Lame Shall Enter First.'" *Flannery O'Connor Bulletin* 2 (1973): 3–18.

Baym, Nina. "Hawthorne's Holgrave: The Failure of the Artist-Hero." *Critical Essays on Hawthorne's* The House of the Seven Gables. Edited by Bernard Rosenthal. Critical Essays on American Literature. New York: G. K. Hall, 1995. 63–75.

———. "Revisiting Hawthorne's Feminism." *Hawthorne and the Real.* Edited by Millicent Bell. Columbus: Ohio State University Press, 2005. 107–24.

———. *The Shape of Hawthorne's Career.* Ithaca NY: Cornell University Press, 1976.

Bell, Millicent. "*The Marble Faun* and the Waste of History." *The Southern Review* 35 (1999): 354–70.

Bercovitch, Sacvan. *The American Jeremiad.* Madison: University of Wisconsin Press, 1978.

Brinkmeyer, Robert. *The Art and Vision of Flannery O'Connor.* Baton Rouge: Louisiana State University Press, 1989.

Brodhead, Richard H. Introduction. In *The Marble Faun*, by Nathaniel Hawthorne. New York: Penguin, 1990. ix–xxix.

Budick, Emily. *Engendering Romance: Women Writers and the Hawthorne Tradition 1850–1990.* New Haven CT: Yale University Press, 1994.

———. "Hester's Skepticism, Hawthorne's Faith; or, What Does a Woman Doubt? Instituting the American Romance Tradition." *Nathaniel Hawthorne's* The Scarlet Letter. Updated ed. Bloom's Modern Critical Interpretations. New York: Bloom's Literary Criticism—Infobase Publishing, 2007. 83–94.

Burns, Shannon. "The Literary Theory of Flannery O'Connor and Nathaniel Hawthorne." *Flannery O'Connor Bulletin* 7 (1978): 101–13.

Butcher, S.C. *Aristotle's Theory of Poetry and Fine Art: With a Critical Text and Translation of* The Poetics. 4th ed. New York: Dover, 1951.

Caron, Timothy P. *Struggles over the Word: Race and Religion in O'Connor, Faulkner, Hurston, and Wright*. Macon GA: Mercer University Press, 2000.

Chase, Richard. *The American Novel and Its Tradition*. New York: Gordian, 1957.

Clarke, Graham. "To Transform and Transfigure: The Aesthetic Play of Hawthorne's *The Marble Faun*." *Nathaniel Hawthorne: New Critical Essays*. Edited by A. Robert Lee. London: Vision Press, 1982.

Coale, Samuel Chase. *In Hawthorne's Shadow: American Romance from Melville to Mailer*. Lexington: University Press of Kentucky, 1985.

Desmond, John F. *Risen Sons: Flannery O'Connor's Vision of History*. Athens: University of Georgia Press, 1987.

Driskell, Leon D., and Joan T. Brittain. *The Eternal Crossroads: The Art of Flannery O'Connor*. Lexington: University Press of Kentucky, 1971.

Edmondson, Henry T. III. *Return to Good and Evil: Flannery O'Connor's Response to Nihilism*. New York: Lexington, 2002.

Emerson, Ralph Waldo. "Nature." *Five Essays on Man and Nature*. Edited by Robert E. Spiller. New York: Harlan, 1957. 1–40.

Feeley, Kathleen. *Flannery O'Connor: Voice of the Peacock*. New Brunswick NJ: Rutgers University Press, 1972.

Feidelson, Charles, Jr. "The Scarlet Letter." *Hawthorne's Centenary Essays*. Edited by Roy Harvey Pearce. Columbus: Ohio State University Press, 1964. 31–77.

Fodor, Sarah. "'A world apparently without comment' or Shouting at the Reader: Narrative Guidance in O'Connor's Fiction." *Flannery O'Connor and the Christian Mystery*. Edited by John J. Murphy. Provo UT: Brigham Young University, 1997. 217–29.

Fogle, Robert. *Hawthorne's Fiction: The Light and the Dark*. Norman: University of Oklahoma Press, 1952.

Frye, Northrop. *The Secular Scripture: A Study of the Structure of Romance*. Cambridge MA: Harvard University Press, 1976.

Gadamer, Hans-Georg. *Truth and Method*. Translated by Joel Weinsheimer and Donald G. Marshall. New York: Crossroad, 1991.

Gentry, Marshall Bruce. *Flannery O'Connor's Religion of the Grotesque*. Jackson: University Press of Mississippi, 1986.

Gordon, Mary. "Is Flannery O'Connor a Catholic?" *Flannery O'Connor Review* 2 (2003–2004): 1–3.

Gordon, Sarah. *The Obedient Imagination*. 2000. Athens: University of Georgia Press, 2003.

Hawthorne, Nathaniel. *The American Notebooks*. Vol. 8, *The Centenary Edition of the Works of Nathaniel Hawthorne*. Edited by William Charvat, Roy

Harvey Pearce, and Claude M. Simpson. Columbus: Ohio State University Press, 1972.

———. "The Birth-mark." *Mosses from an Old Manse.* Vol. 10, *The Centenary Edition of the Works of Nathaniel Hawthorne.* Edited by William Charvat, Roy Harvey Pearce, and Claude M. Simpson. Columbus: Ohio State University Press, 1974. 36–56.

———. *The Blithedale Romance and Fanshawe.* Vol. 3, *The Centenary Edition of the Works of Nathaniel Hawthorne.* Edited by William Charvat, Roy Harvey Pearce, and Claude M. Simpson. Columbus: Ohio State University Press, 1964.

———. "The Celestial Rail-road." *Mosses from an Old Manse.* Vol. 10, *The Centenary Edition of the Works of Nathaniel Hawthorne.* Edited by William Charvat, Roy Harvey Pearce, and Claude M. Simpson. Columbus: Ohio State University Press, 1974. 186–206.

———. "The Custom House." *The Scarlet Letter.* Vol. 1, *The Centenary Edition of the Works of Nathaniel Hawthorne.* Edited by William Charvat, Roy Harvey Pearce, and Claude M. Simpson. Columbus: Ohio State University Press, 1962.

———. "Earth's Holocaust." *Mosses from an Old Manse.* Vol. 10, *The Centenary Edition of the Works of Nathaniel Hawthorne.* Edited by William Charvat, Roy Harvey Pearce, and Claude M. Simpson. Columbus: Ohio State University Press, 1974. 381–404.

———. "Ethan Brand." *The Snow Image and Uncollected Tales.* Vol. 11, *The Centenary Edition of the Works of Nathaniel Hawthorne.* Edited by William Charvat, Roy Harvey Pearce, and Claude M. Simpson. Columbus: Ohio State University Press, 1974. 83–102.

———. *The French and Italian Notebooks.* Vol. 14, *The Centenary Edition of the Works of Nathaniel Hawthorne.* Edited by William Charvat, Roy Harvey Pearce, and Claude M. Simpson. Columbus: Ohio State University Press, 1980.

———. *The House of the Seven Gables.* Vol. 2, *The Centenary Edition of the Works of Nathaniel Hawthorne.* Edited by William Charvat, Roy Harvey Pearce, and Claude M. Simpson. Columbus: Ohio State University Press, 1965.

———. *The Marble Faun.* Vol. 4, *The Centenary Edition of the Works of Nathaniel Hawthorne.* Edited by William Charvat, Roy Harvey Pearce, and Claude M. Simpson. Columbus: Ohio State University Press, 1968.

———. Preface to *The House of the Seven Gables.* Vol. 2, *The Centenary Edition of the Works of Nathaniel Hawthorne.* Ed. William Charvat, Roy Harvey Pearce, and Claude M. Simpson. Columbus: Ohio State University Press, 1965.

————. *"Rappaccini's Daughter." Mosses from an Old Manse.* Vol. 10, *The Centenary Edition of the Works of Nathaniel Hawthorne.* Edited by William Charvat, Roy Harvey Pearce, and Claude M. Simpson. Columbus: Ohio State University Press, 1974. 91–128.

————. *The Scarlet Letter.* Vol. 1, *The Centenary Edition of the Works of Nathaniel Hawthorne.* Edited by William Charvat, Roy Harvey Pearce, and Claude M. Simpson. Columbus: Ohio State University Press, 1962.

————. "Young Goodman Brown." *Mosses from an Old Manse.* Vol. 10, *The Centenary Edition of the Works of Nathaniel Hawthorne.* Edited by William Charvat, Roy Harvey Pearce, and Claude M. Simpson. Columbus: Ohio State University Press, 1974. 74–90.

Heidegger, Martin. *Basic Writings: From* Being and Time (1927) *to* The Task of Thinking (1964). Edited by David Farrell Krell. New York: Harper, 1977.

Hudson, Deal W. "Marion Montgomery and 'The Risk of Prophecy.'" *Thought* 67 (1992): 240–56.

Husserl, Edmund. *Ideas: General Introduction to Pure Phenomenology.* Trans. by W.R. Boyce Gibson. New York: MacMillan, 1931.

Johansen, Ruthann Knechel. *The Narrative Secret of Flannery O'Connor: The Trickster as Interpreter.* Tuscaloosa: University of Alabama Press, 1994.

Keller, Jane Carter. "The Figures of the Empiricist and the Rationalist in the Fiction of Flannery O'Connor." *Arizona Quarterly* 28 (1972): 263–73.

Kevorkian, Martin. "'Within the Domain of Chaos': Nathaniel Hawthorne, Lucretian Physics, and Martial Logic." *Studies in the Novel* 31 (1999): 178–201.

Kohak, Erazim. *Idea and Experience: Edmund Husserl's Project of Phenomenology in* Ideas 1. Chicago: University of Chicago Press, 1978.

Lake, Christina Bieber. *The Incarnational Art of Flannery O'Connor.* Macon GA: Mercer University Press, 2005.

Linge, David E. Introduction. In *Philosophical Hermeneutics,* by Hans-Georg Gadamer. Translated by David E. Linge. 1976. Berkeley: University of California Press, 1977. xi–lviii.

MacKay, Carol Hanbery. "Hawthorne, Sophia, and Hilda as Copyists: Duplication and Transformation in *The Marble Faun." Browning Institute Studies: An Annual of Victorian Literary and Cultural History* 12 (1984): 93–120.

Magee, Rosemary, M., ed. *Conversations with Flannery O'Connor.* Literary Conversations Series. Jackson: University Press of Mississippi, 1987.

Martin, Carter. *The True Country: Themes in the Fiction of Flannery O'Connor.* Kingsport TN: Vanderbilt University Press, 1968.

Martin, Terence. *Nathaniel Hawthorne.* Rev. ed. Boston MA: Twayne, 1983.

Marx, Leo. *The Machine in the Garden: Technology and the Pastoral Ideal in America.* New York: Oxford University Press, 1964.

Matthiessen, F. O. *American Renaissance*. New York: Oxford University Press, 1941.

Montgomery, Marion. "Flannery O'Connor: Realist of Distances." *Realist of Distances: Flannery O'Connor Revisited*. Edited by Karl-Heinz Westarp and Jan Nordby Gretlund. Aarhus, Denmark: Aarhus University Press, 1987. 227–35.

―――. *The Prophetic Poet and the Spirit of the Age*. 3 vols. LaSalle IL: Sugden, 1981–1984.

Nussbaum, Martha C. *The Fragility of Goodness: Luck and Ethics in Greek Tragedy and Philosophy*. New York: Cambridge University Press, 1986.

O'Connor, Flannery. *The Collected Works*. Edited by Sally Fitzgerald. New York: Library of America, 1988.

―――. *The Habit of Being: Letters of Flannery O'Connor*. Edited by Sally Fitzgerald. New York: Farrar, Straus and Giroux, 1979.

―――. *Mystery and Manners*. Edited by Sally and Robert Fitzgerald. New York: Farrar, Straus and Giroux, 1969.

O'Gorman, Farrell. *Peculiar Crossroads: Flannery O'Connor, Walker Percy, and Catholic Vision in Postwar Southern Fiction*. Baton Rouge: Louisiana State University Press, 2004.

Pearce, Howard. "Flannery O'Connor's Ineffable 'Recognitions.'" *Genre* 6 (1973): 298–312.

―――. *Human Shadows Bright as Glass: Drama as Speculation and Transformation*. Lewisburg PA: Bucknell University Press, 1997.

Plato. *The Republic*. Trans. by Paul Shorey. 2 vols. The Loeb Classical Library 237 and 276. Cambridge MA: Harvard University Press, 1982–1987.

Pochmann, Henry A. *Masters of American Literature*. New York: MacMillan, 1949.

Rosenberg, Liz. "'The Best That Earth Could Offer': 'The Birthmark,' A Newlywed's Story." *Studies in Short Fiction* 30 (1993): 145–51.

Rubin, Louis D., Jr. "Flannery O'Connor's Company of Southerners: Or 'The Artificial Nigger' Read As Fiction Rather Than Theology." *Flannery O'Connor Bulletin* 6 (1977): 47–71.

Schiller, Emily. "The Choice of Innocence: Hilda in *The Marble Faun*." *Studies in the Novel* 26 (1994): 372–91.

Shumaker, Conrad. "A Daughter of the Puritans": History in Hawthorne's *The Marble Faun*." *New England Quarterly* 57.1 (1984): 65–83.

Sewall, Richard. *The Vision of Tragedy*. New Haven CT: Yale University Press, 1980.

Strickland, Edward. "The Penitential Quest in 'The Artificial Nigger.'" *Studies in Short Fiction* 25 (1988): 453–59.

Sykes, John D., Jr. *Flannery O'Connor, Walker Percy, and the Aesthetic of Revelation*. Columbia: University of Missouri Press, 2007.

Thoreau, Henry David. *The Maine Woods*. Penguin Nature Library. Edited by Edward Hoagland. New York: Penguin, 1988.

———. *Walden*. New York: Penguin, 1983.

———. "Walking." *The Essays of Henry D. Thoreau*. Edited by Lewis Hyde. New York: Northpoint, 2002. 149–77.

Wagenknecht, Edward. *Nathaniel Hawthorne: The Man, His Tales and Romances*. New York: Continuum, 1989.

Waggoner, Hyatt H. *Hawthorne: A Critical Study*. Rev. ed. Cambridge MA: Belknap-Harvard University Press, 1963.

Wimsatt, William K., Jr., and Cleanth Brooks. *Literary Criticism: A Short History*. New York: Vintage, 1967.

Wood, Ralph C. *Flannery O'Connor and the Christ-Haunted South*. 2003. Grand Rapids MI. Eerdmans, 2004.

———. "Flannery O'Connor's Strange Alliance with Southern Fundamentalists." *Flannery O'Connor and the Christian Mystery.* Ed. John J. Murphy. Provo UT: Brigham Young University, 1997. 75–98.

———. "The Scandalous Baptism of Harry Ashfield: Flannery O'Connor's 'The River.'" *Inside the Church of Flannery O'Connor*. Edited by Joanne Halleran McMullen and John Parrish Peede. Macon GA: Mercer University Press, 2007. 188–204.

———. "Flannery O'Connor, Martin Heidegger, and Modern Nihilism: A Reading of 'Good Country People.'" *Flannery O'Connor Bulletin* 21 (1992): 100–118.

Wray, Virginia F. "Flannery O'Connor in the American Romance Tradition." *Flannery O'Connor Bulletin* 6 (1977): 83–98.

# INDEX

subjectivism, 167–69; on incarnational nature of fiction, 81; influenced by drama, 159–60; insisting on finiteness of human knowledge, 104; linking Catholic dogma and belief with mystery, 154–55; on the Manicheism of the modern mind, 97; on modern consciousness, 80, 90, 93, 98; on modern readers, 84–85; naming Weil and Stein as influences, 155; on the nature of compassion, 104; part of dark tradition of American romance, 9; placing her work in the American romance tradition, 1, 74, 75–76; pointing toward her own incarnational theology, 109; rationalistic worldview of, 80; recommending Heidegger's essays on Holderlin, 138n; religious beliefs of, affecting readers' understanding of her fiction, 130, 154–55; revising Hawthorne's formulation of the romance, 10; sacramental aesthetics of, 8–9; sacramentalism of, 116; sharing beliefs with Hawthorne, 76; similarities of, to Poe and Hawthorne, 9n4; sympathetic to plight of the unbeliever, 88n22; tragedy linked to work of, 160–64; on truth as basis of art, 135; undermining modern rationalism, 5; using historical Southern experience in her romance, 76–77; violence in work of, 165–66; on vision of romance, 74–75; vulgar

touched with sublime in work of, 158–59; work of, likened to tragedies, 171–72; writing with a reasonable use of the unreasonable, 164–65
O'Gorman, Farrell, 88n22
*Our Old Home* (Hawthorne), 176–77
outsider, as hero of modern fiction, 85–86

pastoral idea, 18n10
Pearce, Howard, 160n8
Percy, Walker, 76–77
phenomenology, 156–58
*Pilgrim's Progress* (Bunyan), 114
Plato, 65–66, 134, 161n10, 170n21
play, as metaphor, 132–34
*Poetics* (Aristotle), 66
poor, O'Connor's definition of, 77–78
pornography, 84
pride, danger of, 18
progress, confidence in, 51
Protestant fundamentalism, influence of, on the South, 77
Puritans, 2
Puritans, cosmology of, 41–42; doctrine of, suppressing passional nature, 47; doctrine of natural depravity, 40–41; dualism of, 42–43, 46–47, 57; Hawthorne's feelings toward, 40; idealism of, 55, 63; moral absolutism of, 63–64; religious intolerance of, 41; spiritual and intellectual pride of, 42

"Rappaccini's Daughter" (Hawthorne), 30–33, 35
rationalism, banishing God, 4–5